HELLO FROM
2030

JAN PAUL SCHUTTEN

HELLO FROM
2030

THE SCIENCE OF THE FUTURE AND YOU

ALADDIN
New York London Toronto Sydney New Delhi

BEYOND WORDS
Hillsboro, Oregon

ALADDIN
An imprint of Simon & Schuster
Children's Publishing Division
1230 Avenue of the Americas
New York, NY 10020

BEYOND WORDS
20827 N.W. Cornell Road, Suite 500
Hillsboro, Oregon 97124-9808
503-531-8700 / 503-531-8773 fax
www.beyondword.com

This Beyond Words/Aladdin edition October 2014
English translation copyright © 2014 by Beyond Words/Simon & Schuster, Inc.
Originally published in Belgium in the Flemish language. *Groeten uit 2030* copyright © 2011
by Jan Paul Schutten en Davidsfonds Uitgeverij nv.
Interior illustrations copyright © 2014 by iStockphoto.com
Cover illustration copyright © 2014 by iStockphoto.com

For information about special discounts for bulk purchases, please contact Simon & Schuster
Special Sales at 1-866-506-1949 or business@simonandschuster.com.

The Simon & Schuster Speakers Bureau can bring authors to your live event. For more information
or to book an event, contact the Simon & Schuster Speakers Bureau at 1-866-248-3049 or
visit our website at www.simonspeakers.com.

Managing Editor: Lindsay S. Brown
Editors: Emmalisa Sparrow, Nicole Geiger, Jennifer Weaver-Neist
Translator: Ilse Craane
Design: Sara E. Blum
The text of this book was set in Futura Std.

Manufactured in China 0814 SCP
10 9 8 7 6 5 4 3 2 1

Library of Congress Cataloging-in-Publication Data
Schutten, Jan Paul, author.
   [Groeten uit 2030. English]
   Hello from 2030 : the science of the future and you / Jan Paul Schutten.—
      Beyond Words/Aladdin edition.
   pages   cm
   Audience: Ages 8-12.
   Audience: Grades 3 to 7.
   Includes bibliographical references and index.
   1. Science—Forecasting—Juvenile literature. 2. Technological forecasting—
      Juvenile literature. 3. Social prediction—Juvenile literature. I. Title.
   Q163.S4513 2014
   303.49—dc23
                                                        2013044906
ISBN 978-1-58270-474-6
ISBN 978-1-4814-0946-9 (eBook)

With a special thank-you to Milja Praagman, for coming up with the original title of this book.

Thank you to the professors at KU Leuven, Prof. Ilse Smets, Prof. Herman Bruyninckx, Prof. Wim Dehaene, Prof. Bart Van der Bruggen, Prof. Mélanie Gérard, and Prof. Zeger Debyser, who proofed the text of this book and provided their comments.

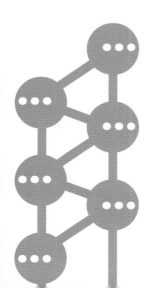

CONTENTS

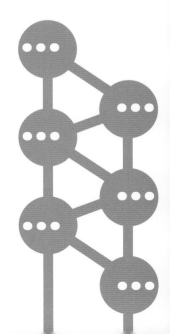

WHY SHOULD YOU BOTHER READING THIS BOOK?

Do you want to laugh? Read this book in 2030! It's full of predictions for the future, and chances are that they are completely wrong. Should you be reading this, then? Of course! Because some of the predictions will come true, and it's good to know what's coming down the road. Even now, we know the Earth's population will grow, our technology is guaranteed to get better, and we will cure more diseases. But other things are less predictable. Maybe there will be an invention that changes everything. Or something will happen that turns the whole world upside down...

> WILD CARDS

The discovery of electricity caused enormous change, just like the invention of computers and the internet. And those things made tons of other innovations possible. In the future, there will certainly be more discoveries and inventions that will change the world. We just don't know what they will be yet.

A future innovation is like the wild card in a card game: you can pull this card at any time and it will change the whole game. An important invention, a new energy source, the end of war are all wild cards. But when you play, there are bad-luck cards as well as wild cards; the bad-luck cards have serious consequences and can cost you the game. Bad-luck cards throughout history have included diseases (like the 14th century bubonic plague), famines, or world wars. These disasters can also happen in the future.

Taking a look into the future can be very exciting, as it can go many different ways. But it's not just exciting, it's important; we *have* to look ahead. We cannot go on living the way we are. If we don't find out now where we will get our power, food, and other resources, we will have huge problems later.

This book won't just give you answers about the future; in the back of it, in the section called "Exercises in Futurology," there will also be questions—questions that will prompt you to think about the future on your own. Sometimes they will be about issues that no one really has a solution for, but they will help you to think about what the future will be like. Perhaps you'll come up with some smart inventions too. You yourself will be an expert of the future! (You can read more about *how* to predict the future in chapter 4, by the way.)

> A MESSAGE FROM 2030

In this book, each chapter starts with a message for you from the year 2030. Sometimes it's from a future that is not doing too great; in other cases, it's from a future where things *are* going great. Both futures are possible. The real future will probably be somewhere in between. Some things will get worse, others will get better. *Probably.* Like someone clever once said, "Prediction is very difficult, especially if it's about the future."[1]

TECHNOLOGY EVERYWHERE

Just before January 1, 2000, millions of people hoped for the best but were worried all the same. Would everything be all right as the new year—the new century—began? Would computers work? Would planes crash? You see, a potentially huge problem threatened to happen: Y2K, or the Millennium Bug.[1] In all electronics, the date was written in short numbers. November 30, 1970, for example, was written as 11-30-70 on a computer chip. At midnight on New Year's Eve, the date was going to be 01-01-00. Lots of electronic appliances would register the date as January 1, 1900, not the first day of the year 2000. And this might cause the appliances to go haywire . . .

> THE DISASTER OF JANUARY 1

The disasters that could happen on January 1, 2000, were inconceivable. Power plants are completely computer operated; would they still work? And what about the nuclear power plants? Would the appliances in hospitals keep working? Modern cars are also full of electronics; would they start? Or airplanes—would their flight computers still work in 2000? And what about automatic teller machines (ATMs)? Would they be out of order, leaving people unable to withdraw money all of a sudden? But also digital watches, DVD players, mobile phones, cameras, ovens and microwaves, satellites, televisions, cooling systems, garage doors, alarms, elevators and escalators, and thousands of other machines could call it quits at any given moment. And if they did, the world would come to a complete and potentially disastrous stop.

Thankfully, it wasn't so bad on January 1, 2000. A few appliances malfunctioned, but in most cases, nothing happened. The world sighed with relief. But it became apparent how much of our world is electronic. This was not the case twenty years before; lots of the electronics in 2000 did not exist in 1980. We're more than ten years past 2000 now, and there are many more new electronics that did not exist then. Technological progress was much faster between 2000 and 2010 than between 1980 and 2000. And it will only get faster. Do the math . . .

> DOUBLEDOUBLEDOUBLE

A thought experiment: You live .25 miles from your school, but for some reason, that distance doubles every day. So the next day, you live .5 miles from your school. The day after, it's 1 mile. Then 2. No problem, you can still ride your bike. By day 5, it's 4 miles; better take the bus. A day later, it's 8 miles, and after that, at one week, it's sixteen miles. And it continues. The next day it's 32 miles; another day later, 64. Day 10 becomes 128. Now you'll have to take a plane, and that's only the beginning. On Day 11, it's 256, then 512, 1024, and after two weeks, you're at 2,048 miles—more than three-fourths of the width of the United States![2] A few days

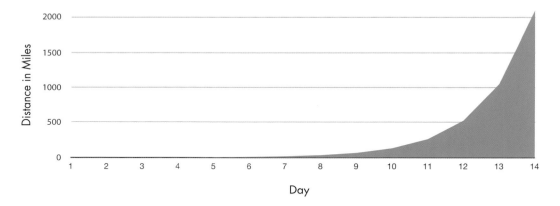

This is a graph of the first days of the thought experiment. Until day 8, things don't seem to be going too fast. But after that? Superfast! The distance on day 17 wouldn't even fit in this book.

into the fourth week, you're at a distance of more than one million miles. That's not even doable with the fastest rocket in the world. After thirty days, the distance has surpassed 134 million, which would be like traveling around the world more than 5,300 times.[3] Three more days, and you've cracked 1 billion miles—a distance that allows you to travel five times to the sun and back![4]

That's the power of doubling. What does that have to do with the future? Everything.

> TO THE MOON WITH AN APP

Our computers know this doubling as well. The first computers were colossal, taking up 1800 square feet,[5] about the size of a small house. And you know what they could do? Almost nothing! The cheapest calculator today is a thousand times faster and better. In fact, according to what is known as "Moore's law," every two years, our computers can

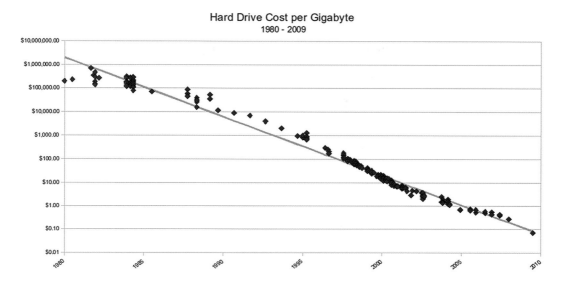

Hard Drive Cost per Gigabyte
1980 - 2009

[Source: Matt Komorowski, "A History of Storage Cost," mkomo.com: http://www.mkomo.com/cost-per-gigabyte (accessed September 12, 2013)]

do twice as much.[6] (I talk more about this in the text box on page 19.) The programs and computer that were needed to get the Apollo 11 to the moon could now be an app on your iPhone. Computers and chips also continue getting cheaper—and at an enormously fast pace. In 1980, a computer with 26 megabytes cost $5,000, or $193 dollars per megabyte. Ten years later, 1 megabyte was only $9; and by the year 2000, it was less than $2. Now? Six cents per gigabyte![7]

> DISPOSABLE COMPUTERS

The progress of computers has enormous consequences for the future. Do you know those greeting cards that make sounds? There is a chip in those cards. And as you've just learned, one of those small chips can do far more than the giant computers from the past. But what do you do with a greeting card like that after a few weeks? You throw it away! A disposable computer—can you imagine the consequences for the future? Because a supersmall computer costs almost nothing, you could put it almost *anywhere*.

Think of foods from the grocery store that beep when they're close to their expiration date. Running shoes that calculate how fast you run, how many calories you burn, and how you can improve your workout. Teacups that tell you when your tea is the right temperature for drinking. Watches with a medical program that informs sick people of their health and when they need to take their medication. The possibilities are endless and will have a major effect on what our world will look like. Where and how we live, for example, will be very different.

MOORE'S LAW

Computers will be, according to a predictable trend, better and cheaper. The person who thought of this is Gordon Moore, a cofounder of Intel, the world's largest semiconductor-chip corporation. In 1964, he discovered the trend that overall processing power will double every two years. His prediction was not entirely correct, so he's had to adjust it a little. But it is still outstanding that he has been right all this time. That's why the law of doubling is named after him.[8] And the best part is that this law doesn't just work for computers. (You'll see what I mean later in this book.)

Hi!

How are you? We just moved! I have a room now that can be as big as one hundred square feet. The room is next to the guest room, and when there aren't any guests, we push my wall out as far as we can so that my room can be extra big. Then, when guests come, we just push the wall back and the guest room is bigger again.

1.
A TOUR OF
YOUR NEW
HOME

My wall is almost seven feet high and twenty feet wide, and made of ePaper. Oh yeah, you don't know what an ePaper wall is. It's a big, thin, three-dimensional screen. Great for watching movies, playing games, or having as a background. You know what? Read this chapter. You'll get to know all about homes in 2030.

A comfortable hello from 2030!

> WELCOME!

What does the house of the future look like? There's a lot of conversation about that among architects. According to some, we won't be living much differently in 2030 than we do now. But according to others, in a few years, homes will have totally different shapes, will be made from completely new materials, and will be filled, of course, with the latest technological gadgets. Other experts say homes won't be made from newly invented materials but from natural stuff: walls of clay where vegetables and fruit can grow, for example.[1] These are three very different ideas that are all very logical. Older homes will continue to be the way they are, but modern homes will change the most. They'll become more environmentally friendly and power efficient. And that can be done in two ways: with natural materials and with high-tech materials.

ARCHITECTURE 2030

So, where did this 2030 milestone come from anyway? What's the big deal about this year?

In 2002, American architect Edward Mazria founded Architecture 2030, a nonprofit, nonpartisan organization dedicated to the global challenge of creating green, carbon-imprint-free structures by the year 2030. This includes the construction of housing, public buildings, and other structures in the building sector, and targets the work of architects, city planners, and governments alike. Architecture 2030 perpetuates its mission through research, education, and open discussion.[2]

> THE LIVING HOME

To build a house today, you get your resources—like wood and stone—from nature. Water flows from the ground through water pipes to your home. And to heat your home, you use wood, gas, oil, or electricity. That's how it is now, and that's how it's always been. But what if you changed that? What if the house provided its own material, water, and power? Materials engineers are working on it!

In the future, you could have a house with walls of earth in which plants can grow. And you'd prune those plants and use the clippings for raw materials—materials to build a wall for another house, for instance. Or you'd use them to fix an existing wall. But you'd use other plants for power.

The leaves of plants are like little power plants that, by way of photosynthesis, turn sunlight into power.[3] They aren't as effective as solar panels but every bit helps. If you also use them to generate electricity, you're using the sun much more effectively. And of course, you use all the rainwater that the house collects for watering these plants. This water is also perfectly suitable for showering, doing the dishes, or flushing the toilet. The rest you filter to use as drinking or cooking water. On your roof, there is also a vegetable garden with a retractable greenhouse, where you cultivate delicious vegetables all year round.

> THE SMART HOME

Another possibility is a house made of plastic or high-tech materials. That doesn't sound too good for the environment, but if those materials last a long time and make it so you don't use a lot of power, then they are suitable. (Dark colors retain heat and whites redirect the heat. Put on a black t-shirt and go sit in the sun; then try a white t-shirt. You'll notice the difference right away.) What do you think about walls that can change like the skin of a chameleon? With cold weather, the walls would become dark and take as much warmth from the light as they can; then, with warm weather, the walls become a cooling white. And cleaning won't be necessary, as the walls would have a self-cleaning outer layer.

The house, of course, also catches the sunlight with the best solar panels. They will be much better in the coming years than they are now. Lots of people think solar panels are extremely ugly, so solar-power engineers are working on changing their shape. One idea is to give them the look of ivy leaves or leaves on a tree.[4] With these solar panels, you could heat water during the summer and store it underground in a big tank to flow through the heating and cooling system, to warm your house in winter. This same tank could also store cold water from the winter to cool your house in summer.

> A TOUR

Want to take a tour of the home of the future? Here we go! You go in through the front door; that will never change. But the door and the lock have changed. In the future, you don't forget your keys anymore because you don't need them; your house simply recognizes you. You're let in, just like that. There is no longer a keyhole that thieves can pick open, which makes the house a lot safer. Should an intruder come in, you're warned right away. Cameras inside your home send images of the intruder to your watch or phone. If it's Grandma, you don't have to worry. But if it's a stranger, you can warn the police with one push of a button.

Cleanliness Is Next to Godliness

When you come in, you notice right away that it's less messy than our homes now. Are we so much tidier in the future? No, there's just less stuff. You don't have a television or stereo anymore because your computer has taken over all tasks. There are also no more DVDs or CDs; all music, movies, shows, and games are available for listening, watching, and playing though the internet (something that's already starting to happen now with online services like Netflix). No more newspapers and magazines are lying about, and hardly any mail is delivered. There will also be far fewer books, as you'll read mostly electronically. (Can you say iPad and Kindle?)

You won't see wires anywhere either. Lamps and electronics work on batteries that last a long time and charge super quickly. Or they have wireless power, like an electric toothbrush. And scattered-around toys? These will probably still be around but much less so than in the past. Computer games are so spectacular that they replace most toys. When you have to clean your room, chances are that you only have to put away some clothes. But maybe your robot does that for you . . .

COMPUTER PAPER
(OR ELECTRONIC PAPER)

As computer chips become smaller and more powerful, allowing them to be put into almost *anything*, display screens will also become smaller and capable of more. And if you combine super-small chips with an ultrathin display screen, you'll have a computer almost as thin as a sheet of paper—a computer that you can fold or roll up and take everywhere with you.[5]

Imagine a few of these sheets as a newspaper or a magazine. The mail carriers and paperboys won't have to come by to deliver printed copies anymore, and the latest editions will appear on your ePaper with great advantages. There will no longer be a need to cut down trees for all those millions of newspapers and magazines; newspapers and magazines will show moving images and have sound just like computers; and every newspaper will bring you the latest news in real time, as it's happening, instead of the next day. Are you on vacation? No problem. You can still download the latest issue of your magazine. And your reading experience won't change much; you can still leaf through the pages. They're just ePaper pages.

The paper is smart too. Put two sheets next to each other, and they will complement each other while creating a screen that's twice as big. Put more sheets together on a wall, and you can change your whole wall into a computer screen. With a remote-control keyboard or speech commands, you can have your computer do exactly what you want:

> Are you playing a racing game? Your wall becomes the windshield of your racecar.

> Want to see a video by your favorite performer? The wall changes your room into a concert hall.

> Call your friends? No! Too boring. You'll video call or Skype. Thanks to the ePaper screens and cameras in each home, it's like you're in the room together.

> Tired of your view? Change your ePaper to display a mountain range!

> Are you sick? With a camera in the classroom, you can still join your class from bed.

A Peek in the Kitchen

The kitchen of 2030 is different too. Here again, the computer plays an important role. A computer with a display screen hangs on the wall, allowing you to watch the news while cooking, listen to music, or watch a cooking video—a video that shows you step by step what to do. That's assuming you still want to cook, because there are delicious—and nutritious—ready-made meals freshly prepared *by your kitchen appliances*![6] All the items in your pantry also house little chips so the kitchen computer knows what you have and don't have. This comes in handy when you tell your kitchen from your office what you'd like to eat that evening.

You'll also get some recipe ideas from your kitchen based on the ingredients that you have and that are reaching their expiration date.

Your kitchen computer automatically makes a grocery list for you too. You can buy those groceries yourself in the supermarket, or you can have them delivered. At one time, there were grocery trucks that drove through neighborhoods daily to make deliveries as well as sell anything a regular store would sell, and these are coming back. When you send in your grocery list, the groceries are delivered to your home a few hours later. It takes less power to drive one truck than for everyone to take their car grocery shopping, so it's better for the environment. Simply walking or biking to do your shopping would, of course, be even better.

Cooking is much faster than it used to be, and the microwave has completely disappeared. (It was too slow and didn't make the food tasty enough.) There are new appliances that are much better, cooking food more quickly and efficiently. And the superfast preparation doesn't just make the food tastier and healthier (shorter cooking times preserve more flavor and nutrition), it also takes less power than the old ways. (There is already a device that turns the toughest meat into a deliciously tender meal in four minutes, and potatoes are cooked in less than a minute.[7]) Cooking is also much safer. New stoves bring cold water to a boil in a few seconds, but when you put your hands on the stovetop, it feels cool. You don't burn yourself as easily.[8]

Taking a Bath was Never this Fun!

Even now, we know we have to be more conservative with water. We are using up Earth's fresh water supply faster than our planet's water cycle can replenish it, but we are already making efforts to conserve and will do so even more in the coming years.[9] It will have big consequences on the way we take showers and baths. Smart showers will make sure that you use less water while showering without you noticing. The water won't flow down to the sewer but will be collected to use as flush water for the toilet. In some houses, it will be purified so that you can shower with it again the next day.[10]

The most exciting thing in your 2030 bathroom is the mirror. You guessed it: it will also be a computer. You can go online and watch your favorite show while brushing your teeth. Or you can go through your calendar and review your appointments for the next day. And you won't be bored taking a bath.

All these changes to our homes in 2030 sound far away. In reality, they will go beyond this because almost all the appliances in this chapter already exist. The question is not whether they can be made; the question is: When will the technology be good enough and affordable enough for everyone to use it?

A lot of these future changes concern power use. Why is that?

Hi there!

When you're reading this, there are seven billion people on Earth. But as of today, on August 8, 2030, there are about eight billion.[1] Eight billion people who all need to live, eat, and drink. And they all need power, which we're barely managing to supply. Our most common sources of energy like coal and gas can't be replaced and are running low. And other alternative sources like solar and wind power do not supply enough, so we need to be very frugal. A much bigger problem is the Earth's climate. Earth has warmed up significantly and has caused

2.
SPACESHIP EARTH

giant deserts to form. The weather is also out of control. Sometimes it doesn't rain for months and other times it doesn't stop for months. And since last year, we've developed another problem: terrorists almost blew up a nuclear power plant. If the authorities had not been able to stop them at the last minute, there would have been a lot of victims. Everyone is scared that the terrorists will try again and succeed.

A concerned hello from 2030 . . .

> A SPACE JOURNEY FULL OF PROBLEMS

Imagine: You're traveling with a group of people to the planet Smurk III. The journey takes thirty years, and you have enough fuel for thirty years. Then your tank will be empty. But the journey is very boring. So everyone on board is playing computer games, and the television is on all day. This really can't go on because the electricity comes from the fuel that you need for the spaceship's engine. Now the fuel will be gone halfway through the journey. Yet everyone happily continues playing and watching, even though it's extremely dangerous. What now? (Do you get what this story is about?)

Someone discovers that there is space dust everywhere that you can turn into fuel. With this dust, you can get some extra time; it works fine. The only problem is that since the dust is being used as fuel, it is getting warmer in the spaceship. The temperature in the spaceship can't get too high or the engine will stop working. (Sound familiar?)

Many different passengers come up with solutions. A sporty passenger has the idea to generate electricity by using dynamos in the fitness room: you can generate power while someone is rowing, biking, or lifting weights. This works but only produces small amounts of power. A plant lover discovers that you can get an electrical current from the plants on board. If you grow more plants, you'll have extra electricity. But this also helps just a little bit—another temporary fix. Someone else finds yet another way to produce electricity: you can crush space rocks and use them as fuel, but this releases a toxic gas. Though you can generate a lot of power with these space rocks, you have to contain the gas so it *never* gets out.

So, what now? Everyone on board has a different plan, but nobody has the perfect solution.

> SPACESHIP EARTH

You figured it out of course. That spaceship is our Earth. The fuel is oil and gas. The space dust is coal. The dynamos and plants are windmills and solar power. The space rocks represent nuclear power. And the opinions on Earth are just as divided as in the spaceship; nobody has a solution that others are satisfied with. It remains a big mystery: Where will we get our power from in the future?

Now imagine you are the secretary of energy. You have to decide where we will get our power until 2030; you have to choose between simple energy sources that are bad for the environment or sustainable energy sources that may only provide temporary fixes. To make sure you have all the right information, you first listen carefully to your advisors:

Oil

Mr. Oil B. Goode: *Oil is by far the best energy source. Almost all our cars use gasoline that is made from oil, and we have a vast supply.*

Ms. Skep Tyck: *A vast supply?! A supply that is diminishing quickly, you mean! If we continue this way, it'll be gone by 2040.*

Goode: *People have been saying that for years. In 1970, they predicted that there wouldn't be any oil left in 2000;[2] now we have more than ever. And our cars are more efficient than they were before. Maybe we'll have enough oil until the year 2100.[3]*

Tyck: *You don't know that. What we do know is that we will run out. And then? Besides, oil is bad for the environment. Our Earth is warming up and what about those oil spills in the ocean?*

Goode: *It's not proven that the Earth is warming up. What would you want instead of oil anyway?*

Oil definitely has its disadvantages. It cannot be replaced, so it's definitely running out at whatever rate that it's used, and it's not good for the environment. Despite what the last advisor says, the Earth is warming up and the use of oil as an energy source directly contributes to this phenomenon.[4] It's also getting more expensive. Maybe, as the secretary of energy, you'll choose something else. Coal, for instance.

Coal

Mr. Cole Happy: We have enough coal for at least two hundred more years.[5] We can generate all the electricity we need with it.

Ms. Skep Tyck: Coal? Now that's really bad for the environment! It produces a lot of waste. It pollutes the air, and burning it produces a lot of carbon dioxide. Carbon dioxide is the main cause for the Earth's warming up.

Happy: Coal is the cheapest.[6] You can drive electric cars with the electricity produced from coal, and electric cars are better for the environment.

Tyck: Yes, but for that electricity you first have to pollute the environment. That doesn't work in the end.

Happy: That's what we should work on: getting power from coal without polluting the environment. What else could we do?

Yeah. Coal is probably the most polluting energy source. But it is a simple way of generating power. Is there something other than coal or oil? Yes: natural gas.

Natural Gas

Ms. Skep Tyck:
Never mind. That's the
same story as oil and coal:
it's easy to obtain, but at
some point, there is no
more left. And it's not good
for the environment.

Ms. Nat Gas: What else
is there?

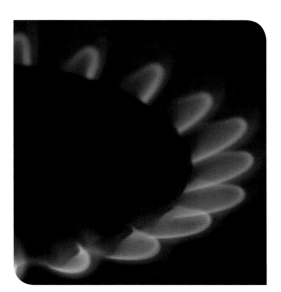

We won't make it with oil, coal, and gas. So, a lot of members of the cabinet choose nuclear power, which is a whole different story.

Nuclear Power

Mr. Nuke Lear: Nuclear
power is fine. It doesn't
pollute, and it's a reliable
source of electricity.

Ms. Skep Tyck: Doesn't
pollute? What about
nuclear waste? Isn't that
pollution?

Lear: We can put that waste away safely. Decades from now, when our technology is more advanced, we'll know what to do with it.

Tyck: Safe? There are all too often accidents with nuclear power plants.

Lear: Yes, but those accidents won't happen with future nuclear power plants.

Tyck: They've been saying that for years, but it still happens. Besides, nuclear power will run out too.

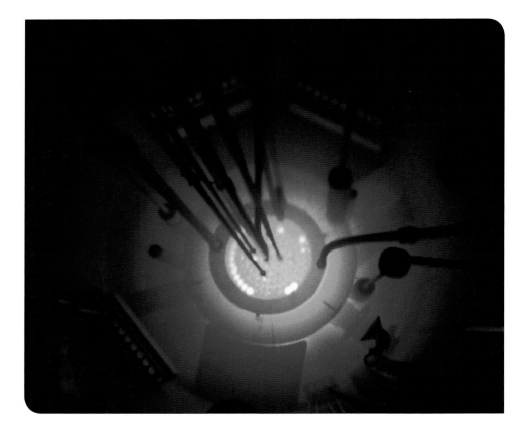

Lear: What do you mean?

Tyck: You need uranium for nuclear power. We don't have a lot of it. At some point, it will run out, just like oil.

Lear: We can use it for at least another half century.[7] And nuclear power doesn't cause the Earth to warm up. What else could you want?

Until now, we've only heard about energy sources that pollute. What about the sustainable sources? Not everything has to be bad for the environment, right? Maybe you'll be the first secretary of energy to choose completely sustainable power.

Biofuel

Ms. Biof Yool: Biofuel is the answer.

Ms. Cure Yus: Biofuel? What's that?

Yool: Natural products like rapeseed oil or corn oil from which you can get energy. They work fine. And they're not harmful to the environment. Did you know you can run a diesel car on frying oil from the supermarket?

Yus: And where do you get this rapeseed oil and corn oil?

Yool: You know—from rapeseed and corn that grows in fields.

Yus: From food?

Yool: Yes.

Yus: But . . . on the other side of the world, people are hungry. Shouldn't you use the food to eat and not to drive a car?

Yool: We've finally found a clean energy source, and it's still not good enough!

Yus: If you want to get enough energy out of crops so that we can all profit from them, you would have to use so much agricultural land that more people will go hungry. Where else would you grow their food?

Yool: We'll think of a solution. What else can we do?

Biomass is being used on a large scale, but it doesn't produce enough power. And it has already caused higher food prices and therefore hunger in poor countries.[8] So, what about wind power?

Wind Power and Hydroelectric Plants

Mr. Gus T. Wind: Wind power. There really is nothing wrong with it.

Ms. Syn Nick: Except that the windmills are ugly, take up too much space, kill birds, and generate too little energy.[9]

Wind: Windmills are improving. We'll get more energy out of them in the future. And if they're so ugly, we can put them at sea. They'll be out of the way, and it's always windy there.

Nick: That's too expensive. Wind power is already more expensive than most other forms of energy.[10] And what if there is no wind?

Wind: It's always windy somewhere. We'll use the energy from the places where it is windy.

Nick: That's too complicated.

Wind: Then we'll use energy from hydroelectric plants. We can turn those on whenever we want.

Nick: Hydroelectric plants?

Wind: Yes, hydroelectric plants are those enormous dams on rivers. You can generate electricity from the pressure of the intercepted water.

Nick: If you add that to wind power, how much do you generate?

Wind: Well, there aren't that many rivers. If all goes well, we can get more than fifty percent of all energy from hydroelectric and wind power.

Nick: So, not enough.

Wind: Maybe with solar power . . .

Solar Power

Mr. Sonny Day: Did you know that the amount of energy the sun sends to the planet is 20,000+ times more than all the energy people use on Earth? An hour of solar power is enough to run all the appliances, lights, and machines on the planet.[11]

Ms. Hope Full: Yes. The only problem is that we have yet to find a good way to convert that energy.

Day: We are getting better at finding ways.

Full: Solar panels cost a lot of money.[12] Besides, you need too much material to make enough solar cells to get enough energy for the whole planet.

Day: Yes, but something special is happening with solar cells.

Full: Oh, really? What?

Day: Moore's law applies to solar power.

Full: What's that again?

Day: Doubling. Solar cells are getting better and cheaper. If it continues at the same pace, solar power will be the best and cheapest source of power.

Full: Yes, but will it continue at the same pace in the future?

Day: Most likely.

Full: It's not for sure?

Day: No.

Full: And how much power do we get from the sun now?

Day: Um, well, uh . . . too little.

POWER FROM KITES

Windmills are expensive to make; a lot of power and resources are needed. To earn out the manufacturing cost, it needs to be spinning nonstop for years. Another disadvantage is that the windmills are often located in isolated spaces, far away from the grids that need the electricity most. The question is whether windmills are the right solution for the future.[13]

One of the major problems with windmills is that it's not always windy enough—on Earth anyway. Up high in the sky, however, there is a lot more wind; it would be great if  you could get power from flying kites. And that is actually what they are currently researching and testing.[14] There have been different tests with kites whose flying lines spin a dynamo that produces energy we can use. And when the line is completely rolled out, the kite becomes smaller so it can be pulled back in with little strength.

The inventor, Saul Griffith, is one of the researchers who has developed such a way to get energy from kites. He has already built kites that generate enough power for five households. The bigger the kite, the more power it will generate. And these kites are much more cost effective than windmills: with the constant winds up higher in the sky, they constantly generate power, earning back the cost to build them in no time. According to Griffith, he could provide all of America with electricity if he gets enough funding and space to fly more and bigger kites.[15] Other experts are less optimistic. They expect that successfully getting enough energy from kites won't happen until after 2020.

> WANTED: CLEAN ENERGY

Almost all the power sources that we have now and in the future are mentioned above. There are more, but these sources also have their disadvantages. A tough problem—and all the experts contradict each other. Many of their past predictions also turned out to be wrong.

Do you have the right solution?

Currently, most countries choose to use a little bit of everything: oil, coal, gas, and nuclear supplemented with sustainable sources. But eventually, the sustainable sources will become more important. Not only will their technology improve to generate more energy but they will be required to do so. Oil will become more scarce and more expensive. There will also be more people on Earth who will use that energy. To have enough power in the future, we have to make sure that we generate a lot of extra energy in addition to what we currently produce. How much? *A lot*—seventeen times more than all the nuclear power plants on Earth right now.[16]

Think of how many more electrical appliances we have now compared to twenty years ago. Now think of how many more we'll have in 2030, and how much power we'll need to keep all those cars, air conditioners, washing machines, and newly invented appliances running. Our quest for sustainable, clean energy continues!

CLEAN ENERGY FOREVER

You (Secretary of Energy): Is there not one sustainable power source that could produce enough energy?

Ms. X. Pert: Yes, there is.

You: Is that a source that will last forever?

Pert: Absolutely.

You: Well, what is it?

Pert: Fusion power.

You: What's that?

Pert: Take a deuterium isotope and a tritium isotope and you meld them with a helium isotope. Then . . .

You: Okay, okay, okay, that's enough. Have we generated power with fusion before?

Pert: Yes, regularly.

You: What is the problem, then? Why don't we have dozens of fusion power plants?

Pert: Because fusion only happens at very high temperatures.

You: How high?

Pert: About 150 million degrees.

You: Whew.

Pert: You can say that again. It's been possible to generate energy with fusion for some time, but it takes much more power than it produces.[17]

You: So, to turn on a lightbulb with fusion power, you need one hundred light bulbs.

Pert: Pretty much.

You: Why do we even try?

Pert: Because it might be possible one day to make fusion happen at lower temperatures.

You: Do scientists think it will ever work?

Pert: Most are certain it will.

You: And do they know when it will happen.

Pert: No. Some think it will happen within thirty years.

You: But . . . ?

Pert: They said forty years ago that they could do it in thirty years . . .

You: So what do we do now?

Pert: Scientists are continuing their research. Maybe there will be a breakthrough in a few years. That will be the biggest news since the internet.

Fusion power is not the only wild card. There are many other technologies that could end the energy problem.[18] Like power from algae and seaweed. Or tide power: using the massive hydro-power from the ocean's tides. Power from the sea's waves. Power from the heat of the Earth's core. Imagine if we could generate power from lightning bolts. As soon as someone finds an appropriate way to effectively use these technologies, we'll never have to worry about our power usage again.

> SHOULD WE WORRY?

Where will we get all this power that we need in the future? Even the greatest scholar on Earth can't give us a clear answer. But we don't have to fear that we will be without electricity in a few years. There is enough for the time being. Besides, there is one more way to control our energy supply: be energy efficient.

Of course, improvements in technology help. More than fifty years ago, a Volkswagen Bug drove thirty miles to a gallon; the newest Volkswagens get at least twice as much per gallon.[19] And there are cars that drive ninety-five miles with that gallon! The world's cleanest car made it 8,914 miles with just one gallon![20] We'll break that record a few more times in the coming years. Electric appliances will also become more efficient, and that makes a big difference. So, we'll still have power in the future—but the same can't be said for a clean environment or stable global temperatures.

THE MOST LOGICAL SOLUTION IS NOT ALWAYS THE BEST

You live in a new house with a big garden. In the summer, it's very warm in the sunshine. What do you do? You buy a parasol. Logical. But your neighbor does something else. He plants a few apple seeds. He gives them water and takes care of them. Over the next few summers, you're in the shade while your neighbor is watering his small apple trees. But after ten years, the roles have reversed. You have to get out the parasol every time the sun shines and buy a new one when it breaks or wears out. But the neighbor has shade every day from his trees. And in the fall, he has delicious apples.

It's the same story with our energy supply. Sure, there are solutions for the future. However, the sooner we do our research, the more we can benefit from them. But we want a solution now, and most of us don't think of the future. That's why we still use so much oil, gas, and coal, and don't work hard enough on the other energy sources.

> IS THE EARTH WARMING UP?

You don't feel very well and go to the doctor. Actually, you don't go to one doctor, you go to a hundred. Of the hundred doctors, ninety-five say that you are sick: the next few years you'll be okay, they say, but you'll continue to get sicker until you get a new liver. Meanwhile, there are five other doctors who are just as good but say there is nothing wrong with you. According to them, you'll be fine. What do you do? And when do you act—right away? Or do you wait?

Scientists think the same way about the Earth warming up as the doctors do about your body. Most agree that the Earth is warming, and most even say that it is most certainly because of our energy use: The burning of oil and gas allows carbon dioxide and methane to enter the air. Then the gases rise above the clouds and create a kind of screen around the Earth that holds in the warmth generated by the sun. That's why they are called greenhouse gasses. With our current use of energy, there will be more greenhouse gases raising the Earth's temperature, which in turn can cause gigantic environmental disasters.[21] According to serious predictions, average global temperatures will be ten degrees (Fahrenheit) warmer by the year 2100,[22] and the consequences will be noticeable. Some areas have already had terrible droughts for years, where other regions have had too much rain.

> WHAT ARE THE CONSEQUENCES OF A WARMER EARTH?

The weather and the climate are exceptionally complicated. So it's difficult to predict what will happen as the Earth warms up. But a few things will certainly happen. A lot of ice on land will melt and run into the sea. The sea level will rise and low-lying areas will disappear under water. Tens of millions of people will have to move. Large agricultural areas will be useless because of drought. The areas where it is already too dry will dry out further. The weather will also become more extreme. More rain, cold, and heat records will be broken.[23] Maybe it will be 70 degrees in December and it will snow in May. The weather could be so strange that even with a warming climate, it may be extraordinarily cold in certain areas.

> THE SOLUTION?

Back to the story about your liver. Would you immediately undergo a complicated and risky operation? Would you wait a while, or would you do nothing? Most countries are waiting to make any big decisions. They continue to use lots of oil, gas, and coal, and hope that it won't be so bad in the future, when there are more sustainable sources. In the coming years, we will send more carbon dioxide and methane into the atmosphere than ever before. If the scientists are right, the Earth will warm up at a fast rate. Or is there another solution?

Imagine you are still using lots of oil and coal, but at the same time, something takes place that brings down the Earth's temperature. This is possible; we see it happen sometimes. And it's not people who do it but the Earth itself. When a volcano erupts, there is so much ash in the upper layers of the atmosphere that the temperature on Earth goes down. Volcanic ash stops some sunlight, and also causes more clouds and rain.[24]

What a volcano can do, people can too. Geoengineers, also known as climate engineers, are working on ways to blow, like a volcano, giant amounts of (artificial) ash into the atmosphere that can cool the Earth. It's technically easy to do, but it's also temporary. The particles fall back down to Earth and the greenhouse gases remain. The problem of global warming could be solved if particles were consistently blown up into the atmosphere, but geoengineers do not know the long-term effects.[25] So they continue to research and test new ways of stopping or slowing down the rising temperatures. And unfortunately, artificial volcanic ash doesn't solve the other problem: pollution. That's a much bigger problem.

Hi!

Perhaps you think that everything will be better in the future. That's correct for the most part, but not for everything— because the world you know no longer exists. Complete rainforests have disappeared. Large sections of the oceans are empty of life. And lots of animals and plants are gone from the Earth. How many?

3.
FROM DIRTY HUMAN TO "GREEN" AS AN ANT

We don't know. A lot of species were gone before they could be studied. Thankfully, things are getting better now. We aren't as careless as we were in the past, and we are much more attentive to our planet. There are plans to plant new rainforests, the last of the coral reefs are well protected, and we don't pollute as much as we used to. Our kids call us crazy for how irresponsible we were with our world. And you know what? They're right.

A sad hello from 2030 . . .

> THE MOST BEAUTIFUL PLACES ON EARTH FOR AS LONG AS THEY EXIST

What is the most beautiful place on Earth? "The coral reefs!" say the people who have been there. They are amazingly colorful underwater landscapes, where you won't just see unbelievably striking corals but also the most magnificent fish. It's those coral reefs that are most at risk of disappearing in the near future.

Coral is extremely sensitive to the Earth's rising temperature, as well as greenhouse gases. Carbon dioxide is not only polluting the air, it's also in the water. The reefs are already diminishing, and according to some predictions, they will be reduced to half their size within twenty-five years. In addition to the coral, the fish and other animals that live on and near the reefs will have disappeared.[1]

> TREES AND ANIMALS

Will people let it go this far? Definitely. It has happened before. Currently, we only have half of the forests that we used to have (before humans and deforestation), and the forests continue to be destroyed at a rapid pace. In the time that it takes you to read these sentences (about a minute), forests the size of thirty-six football

fields were felled. That's 46–58 million square miles of forest harvested every year![2]

Here goes one field. And another. And another. Thankfully, there is still plenty of forest, but you understand that, at this rate, there will be very little left.

But why are these forests cut down? Why is no one stopping it? First, much of the forest is cut down to create agricultural land. Forests are profitable when the timber is harvested to make houses, furniture, or paper, but agricultural fields make a profit year after year. You can put cows on them, or grow soybean plants and palm trees. Soy and palm oils are important ingredients in countless food products. Of course, the lumber is worth something too—to make houses, furniture, or paper, for instance.

Not only the trees but also the animals that live there will vanish when these forests are cut down. In the rain forests, for example, various species will live around one tree—squirrels, monkeys, birds, bats, moths, beetles, flies, lice, and other insects—too many to name. When the tree disappears, these species lose their habitat, food, and protection from predators. Moreover, trees process a lot of carbon dioxide via photosynthesis—the process by which trees grow—and simultaneously supply the oxygen that we need to

breathe. Fewer trees means more carbon dioxide left free in the air. And that negatively affects the corals . . .[3]

ONE PERSON IS STUPID, TWO ARE MORE STUPID

There is a dangerous chain of thought that enters a lot of people's minds: *If this problem is so bad, wouldn't our government do something about it?*

Our government isn't crazy, is it? Its regulators wouldn't let it get that bad? Wouldn't a lot of other people—other countries—say something otherwise? Why don't we hear that much about it? The problem probably isn't that bad.

It is very normal for people to think this, but it is also very risky. You can compare it with what happens when someone falls into a lake. The bystanders all wonder if they should jump in the water to save the person from drowning. While they are thinking, nobody does anything. And because no one is doing anything, they all think: *Hey, everyone else is just watching. Maybe I don't have to do anything either. Doing nothing is probably better because that's what most people are doing.* And so, it has often happened that someone drowns while others watch. If there is only one bystander, the person will almost always jump in and try to help. Psychologists have done all sorts of experiments, and this is usually the case. They call it "group stupidity" or "groupthink."[4]

Group stupidity mostly occurs in situations that are difficult to assess, particularly when people have to make an effort to solve the problem. Problems like energy shortages, environmental pollution, deforestation, and exhaustion of fish stocks all belong to the kinds of issues where group stupidity can occur. Thankfully, the opposite also exists: group wisdom. Makes sense, because two people know more than one. And together, they can think of a better solution than on their own. This is also the case for our future, but it only works if people really work together to find a solution. And that is not always the case.

Earlier

Now

Later

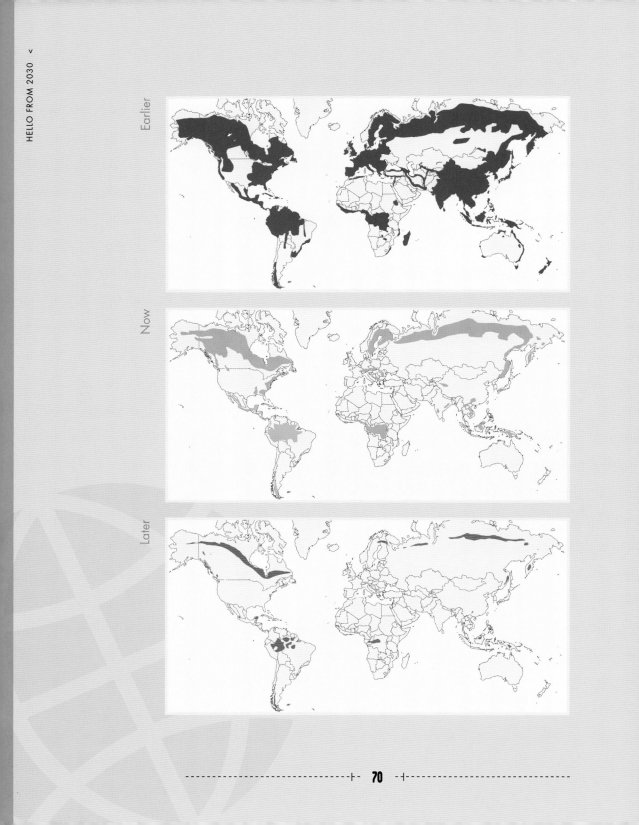

Is there a solution? Can we invent something that stops deforestation and the extinction of the reefs? Can we regrow the coral reef? No. Species that become extinct do not come back. And forests do not grow back on their own; new trees have to be planted. Only governments can do something by prohibiting deforestation and limiting carbon dioxide output, but this is not happening often or fast enough.

> A NEW WAY OF THINKING

Millions of children played with rubber duckies when they were small. To make those duckies, manufactures had to take resources from nature. And from those resources, they made the duckies toxic. On the packaging, it said that children shouldn't hold the duckies in their mouths too long or they would get sick. When the children got older, or if the ducky broke, it was thrown away. It was then tossed into a trash incinerator with lots of other trash, and its toxic ashes ended up in a garbage dump, the toxic gas in the atmosphere. In other words, people took useful resources from nature to make toxic toys that would end up polluting the Earth as waste for years and years. It can't get any more irresponsible; we exhaust one area to pollute another.

> THE DIFFERENCE BETWEEN ANTS AND PEOPLE

A lot of toys are still made this way. Not only toys, but also cars, computers, furniture, clothes, and numerous other objects around us—each one bad for the environment. And the more people, the more we pollute the Earth. Are there just too many of us?

No. Look at ants. If you count all the ants in the world, they carry more environmental impact than all the humans in the world. They eat more than humans, and they even use more land than us. Still, ants are not harmful to the environment. Why not? Because they treat the Earth better than we do. If ants can do it, why can't we?

A REAL-LIFE JURASSIC PARK?

In the movie *Jurassic Park*, scientists found a way to bring back dinosaurs from extinction. They took cells from dinosaur bones, brought them to life, and used them to breed new animals. This is great for a book or a movie, but in reality, it is still completely impossible. The dinosaurs died so long ago that the cells in their bone fossils are too damaged. But with animals that have become extinct later on, it might work . . .[5]

Mammoths, for instance, have been found that have not defrosted since they froze immediately after death so long ago. Those animals are so well preserved that their cell tissues *can* be used. Japanese researchers are now trying to put that cell tissue into an elephant's egg cell.[6] Then they'll put that egg cell into the womb of an elephant and hope that a little mammoth will be born. Whether this will be possible in the next few years is uncertain, but one day, it will happen. The question is whether it should be allowed. What kind of life will that mammoth have, all alone, without any other members of his species? And while he's being examined for hours every day by scientists?

On the other hand, it's a way for extinct animals to return to the world. We can turn back the clock a little and give animals and plants that disappeared another chance—especially those that we caused to disappear fairly recently. It just isn't possible for *everything* that has gone extinct. Forests are vanishing so quickly that there are animals and plants disappearing that we don't even know exist.

> AN INFINITE CIRCLE

This is the challenge thousands of manufacturers are currently working on: Why don't we make products that are good for the environment—that you can use to make other new things? Take clothes, for instance. All clothes wear out or go out of style, and most clothes are made of natural fibers from plants like cotton, flax, bamboo, and hemp. Instead of throwing them away, you would compost them to grow new plants for clothing. This way, you don't pollute, you don't take more resources from nature than you actually need, and you can endlessly make new clothes that follow the latest trends!

This way of making products has been harnessed in a framework called "Cradle to Cradle"; with it, new things that are broken are just in the cradle of being another new thing again.[7] The idea has existed for many years, and more things are now being made this way: clothes, shoes, carpets, furniture, houses. And they're working on cars. This isn't just better for the environment, it's cheaper too. Everyone wins, so more and more companies are interested in this method of production.

It's more easily said than done, however. Everything you make has to be able to be reused as something new and of equal worth. Lots of things can be reused, but their value diminishes. Glass can be melted down to create new glass, for instance, but each time, you are left with less glass. In this case, we call it recycling, and recycling is much better than just throwing it away. But it's still not as good as Cradle to Cradle.

> THE ETERNAL CITY

At this time, there are very few things made as Cradle to Cradle. In the future, however, you'll see it much more. Not only will products be completely reusable but cities will be built according to the same principle.

Buildings, roads, town squares, parks will all be designed in such a way that you can take them apart to make new

things. The city won't take water from the ground but catch rainwater. Dirty water will be cleaned and filtered for reuse. In addition, most of the food for the city's inhabitants will be grown in the city itself. Farmers will have their fields on the roofs of buildings, and enormous tanks under the building will collect and store water like the home you toured in chapter 1. The water that has been heated by the sun in the summer is used to heat the buildings in the winter. Similarly, the cold water from the cooler seasons' snow and rain will be used to cool the buildings in the summer. Solar panels will provide most of the energy.[8] It doesn't get any better than this.

PLASTIC SOUP

Not everything made of plastic ends up in a trash can. When you're outside, you'll often see plastic bags, bottles, and containers lying around—this happens all over the world. And a lot

of that plastic ends up in the ocean. Because plastic doesn't sink, the wind and waves carry it away from shore to collect where the ocean currents meet. All the plastic that was ever littered is still floating around somewhere.

This has caused a "plastic soup" in an enormous area of the ocean. How big? No one knows exactly; it is at least three times as big as California. About two hundred *billion* pounds of garbage are floating between North America and Japan.[9] And then there are other places where billions of pounds are floating as well . . .

Lots of animals like fish and birds eat this plastic and die from it. Several species are threatened with extinction because of it.[10] This is why an increasing number of countries have banned plastics that are only used once. Instead of being made of plastic, packaging will all be biodegradable in a few years. You'll throw it away with the rest of the garbage after you use it, but should it end up in nature, it will become food for the environment.

> EVERYTHING IS RUNNING OUT . . .

Cradle to Cradle might sound like an environmentalist's dream right now, but it isn't. Not only oil and gas but metals like iron, lead, silver, aluminum, and many others are finite natural resources that are running low. And these are not even the most important resources. There are metals like neodymium, lanthanum, dysprosium, and cerium. You've probably never heard of them, but they are used to make cars, computers, iPods, smartphones, and televisions.[11] We can't go without these materials, so we need to be efficient and reuse when we can. The only problem: some of these metals cannot be recycled, so we'll need a solution for that too.

One thing is for sure: in the future, we will be much more environmentally friendly—not because we want to be but because we *have* to be. In a few decades, people will think differently about those strange people at the beginning of the twenty-first century who polluted their planet in the most bizarre ways.

Hi!

You're reading a book right now about the future, but time doesn't stand still, of course. So in 2030, we continue to be concerned about the coming years.

- What new machines and appliances will there be in 2050?

- Will we be getting resources and energy from the moon or other planets?

- Will the world be made up of just a few countries with a few governments?

- Will we have an anti-aging product that allows us to live forever?

4.
HOW DO YOU PREDICT THE FUTURE?

- Will we have the first robots that we cannot immediately distinguish from humans?

It's all possible. But where do these predictions come from? Who thinks of them? How does a predictor work? How do you get useful information from a murky muddle of fuzzy uncertainties?

A curious hello from 2030!

Do you ever read your horoscope in the newspaper? Do you believe what it says? Do you trust people who tell you your future by looking at the lines on your hands, fortune tellers with a crystal ball, or people who can see what will happen to you in a deck of cards? Hopefully not. There are numerous spectacular stories of predictions that came true, but not one has been proven.

There is a man who has promised to pay a million dollars to people who can make important predictions that actually come true. That man, James Randi, used to be a magician, so he knows all the fortune tellers' tricks—and he doesn't trust them for a minute. Hundreds of psychics have gone to him with their predictions, but James Randi still has his million in the bank. Not one psychic has accurately predicted the future.[1]

> CLAIRVOYANTS AND FUTUROLOGISTS

If you want to know what will happen in the future, go to the scientists not the fortune tellers. They can't guarantee that their predictions will come true either, but they at least know more about the subject matter. Researchers who concern themselves with the future are called futurologists, and as a futurologist, you have to keep track of everything. Technology is at the top of the list, of course, because you should know the computer, chip, car, and phone the manufacturers are working on.

But politics are important too. You have to know what decisions governments are making and what resolutions they are making for the future. You need to know biology, geography, and chemistry to understand what is happening to the Earth. And you have to know history, because a lot of things that happened in the past can happen again in the future.

> PREDICTIONS GONE WRONG

Knowledge alone is not enough to say sensible things about the future. You can know a lot about a certain subject but make a completely wrong prediction, which has happened before. Thomas Watson once said that we would only need five computers for the whole world, and Watson wasn't just anybody; he was the CEO of IBM, the only company making computers at the time.[2] In 1949, a *Popular Mechanics* article predicted that there would be computers that weigh less than 3,000 pounds.[3] Well, the writer was right, except that the computers he was referring to now weigh *ten thousand times less* than he predicted. Whether the technology was the computer, radio, television, or phone, there were always experts who knew for sure that no one would ever be interested. There were brilliant scholars who said it would be impossible to fly, let alone send a rocket to the moon. And aren't we glad they were wrong!

NOSTRADAMUS, THE MOST FAMOUS PREDICTOR EVER

About 450 years ago, there lived a man named Nostradamus. He made a lot of remarkable predictions and became world famous because of them. His books have been published in many languages and are still read by thousands of people today.

Nostradamus's predictions were sometimes hundreds of years into the future. According to some, he predicted important events like Napoleon's victories, World War II, and the recent terrorism in Europe. Here is something he once wrote:

Beasts ferocious with hunger will swim across the rivers, greater part of the army will be against Hister.

The great one will cause him to be dragged in a cage of iron, when the German infant observes no law.[4]

It all sounds a bit confusing, but that's how Nostradamus wrote. A lot of his words are meant to be read metaphorically. The "beasts ferocious with hunger" could be soldiers ferocious with hunger. And "Hister" sounds a lot like Hitler, don't you think? "Cages of iron"? Those are likely tanks, which didn't exist at the time of Nostradamus, so he called them cages. And "the German infant" indicates that Hister is from Germany. In short, did Nostradamus predict the advance of tanks against Hitler in World War II?

Some people think so. But this is a translation of a text that is hundreds of years old. And Nostradamus wasn't just confusing, he also wrote in different languages. Sometimes he wrote in French, then Latin or Italian, or even Greek. So you can translate his words in different ways. And yes, if you can read the texts in different ways, then it is easy to adapt them after the fact in such a way that it sounds like the predictions came true. Besides, Nostradamus frequently wrote less vague texts that were clearly not right. A very famous predictor, this Nostradamus, but not a very good one.

> HOW DO YOU PREDICT THE FUTURE?

1: Read, Read, Read, and Think

Knowledge alone is not enough to predict the future; you have to do something with that knowledge. In 1946, film producer and studio owner Darryl F. Zanuck told people that television would be a short trend: "People will soon get tired of staring at a plywood box every night."[5] Less than ten years later, more than half of all US homes had a television.[6] The man didn't take a good look around him. He was in the movie business and didn't think about the potential of television— TV shows, movies, and news, for instance. Advertising. Hundred of channels. A set in every room of the house. Videorecorders. DVRs. On demand. Gaming consoles. Internet television. Had he taken these into account, he never would have said such a silly thing. He didn't concern himself with these details.

A good futurologist reads as many newspapers, magazines, trade journals, and websites as she can to be up to date, and then uses all that information to make a prediction.

2: Make Graphs

If you want to know what role solar power will play in the future, you should really look at the past. What could solar panels do in 1975? And in 1980? And five years after that? You will be able to see at what rate solar panels are improving. You can make a graph to see if there is a certain steady trend to it.

When you look at the graph (like the one below), you'll see that solar panels are generating more energy over the last few years. That improvement is going at a constant rate, and we can assume that this improvement will continue in the coming years. And maybe the years after that too. Sometimes you'll see a line on a graph like that becomes less steep. In that case, the pace of development is slowing down. Or you'll see a line getting steeper, which means a lot more change is happening at an even faster rate.

World Usage of Solar Energy

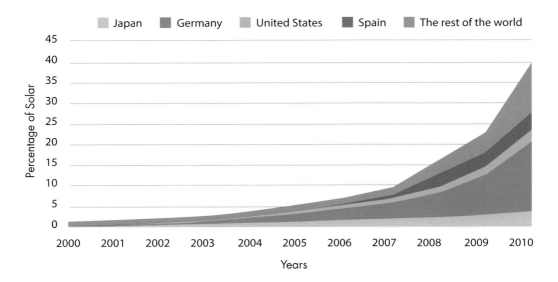

Look at the numbers on the graph over the years and try to predict which way things will go in the future. There are no guarantees for the future, of course, but this method works surprisingly well in most cases.

3: Think It Through

In futurology, you have to think things through. What are the consequences of a certain occurrence or development? And what are the consequences of those consequences?

Imagine that you discover that solar panels will be improved and affordable enough in five years that they will be our primary source of power. A lot will change. All those powerful companies and countries that sell oil won't be so important anymore. Our cars will change because they can drive on solar power. Our homes will change. There will be lots of new companies that have to do with solar panels, while oil companies disappear. Some people will lose their jobs and others will find new ones; one occurrence is the cause of the next occurrence.

If you think about what could happen and what consequences that occurrence will have, you come to all sorts of surprising developments that could be very important in the future.

4: Come Up with Ideas

There are futurologists who primarily work with their imagination. They pose all sorts of questions: What do we need most right now as human beings? What is an invention that we are all waiting for? After they think of something, they research how far technology has advanced in that area: Is it an invention we can expect in the next five years? Ten years? Is there a lot of work being done on it?

This method of prediction is especially complicated. You have to envision machines that do not exist yet. Still, this method delivers interesting results. Jules Verne wasn't a futurologist but a writer, and he came up with all sorts of things that later became a reality, like a submarine and a rocket to the moon. In the TV show *Star Trek*, the characters use a "tricorder," a handheld device that delivers all kinds of information about one's surroundings, including medical readings. To a degree, our smartphones do the same now.[7] In the movie *2001: A Space Odyssey*, the characters have devices that work a lot like iPads.[8] In fact, futurologists usually invite science-fiction writers to their conferences to exchanges ideas about how the future will be.

5: Look At the Past

"*L'histoire se repète*," is the French saying—"history repeats itself." It doesn't happen the same way every time, but it's recognizable enough to say it happened before. Wars, contagious diseases, natural disasters. It seems history rarely repeats the good kind of event, and yet these events can—and will—happen again. Though it's unpleasant to think about, it's important to do so anyway: In what ways can we prevent these events? Where? And what consequences will these interventions have? By studying the past, you can take preventive measures. And this does happen, thankfully. In 1918, there was a flu epidemic so bad that tens of millions of people died.[9] In the last few years, other flu epidemics have also threatened humankind, but knowing what happened in the past has provided people with ways of containing new epidemics, preventing similar catastrophes.

6: Stack Inventions

First there was electricity. Then the telephone. Then came the mobile phone. Then all these apps for phones. You need one invention to get to the other. Some futurologists look at the new technologies that are already here. Then they look at what other technologies will be possible later because of these. After that, they look at what these new inventions make possible.

By stacking inventions, futurologists try to estimate when we can use new technologies. Imagine you know when solar panels will be five times better than they are now. Stack that on top of engines that are three times more energy efficient. Combine that with strong materials that are ultra lightweight and you'll know exactly when there will be planes that fly on solar power.

RAY KURZWEIL: THE FUTUROLOGIST WHO WILL NOT DIE

Ray Kurzweil is an inventor. His first invention, about fifty years ago, was a computer that could compose music. He also thought of a computer that could read text to blind people. And he built computers that could understand spoken language and do what you tell them. But that isn't everything. He thought of dozens of computer programs and devices; as an inventor he has an enormous understanding of technology. And he is confident enough to predict which inventions will be made in the future and when they will take place.[10]

In 1990, he wrote a book about future devices called *The Age of Intelligent Machines*. In the book, he made over a hundred predictions about new devices, and most of them came true. He could even point out which year we would all be using these devices. His predictions were about mobile phones and the internet, and about computers that could beat people at chess—things that are normal now but definitely weren't in 1990.[11]

According to Kurzweil, there is plenty coming our way in the coming years. He strongly believes in Moore's law and thinks inventions will be more spectacular each year.[12]

Think about the following: the first computers were conceived by making notes on paper, without any other help. Only later could we use computers to devise better computers. And those better computers helped us make even better computers. This continues to happen, and our computers become smarter and smarter—until they become more intelligent than ourselves. And then the developments *really* pick up at an incredible rate.

We'll have computers that can conceive of better computers than we could ever build. And these computers will think of solutions to all sorts of problems that our ordinary human intelligence could never have solved. We'll find a way to rejuvenate our bodies. We'll no longer die of old age. There will also be ways to cure various deadly diseases. In short, we'll have become almost immortal. Kurzweil believes this will happen by the year 2045. He will be 97 years old.[13]

It sounds very far away and unbelievable—and it is. Not everyone agrees with Kurzweil. But . . . he has been right before.

> HOW DO YOU KNOW IF A PREDICTION CAN COME TRUE?

Assurances for the future don't exist. And the best futurologists are often wrong. Still, there is a way to test if your idea for the future can come true.

Let's say you would like to know if a certain invention or technology could succeed. A cheap water purifier, for instance. You can ask the following questions:

1: Is the technology almost there? Does the invention depend on one important development that is far off? Are there multiple ways to make the device?

With water purifiers, the answer is yes; you can purify water in several ways. They all have their pros and cons, but the technology keeps improving. And if one method is not making much progress, another might make more of a difference. Sometimes you can combine technologies and make more progress.

2: Will the device be beneficial? Is it really useful? Is it of interest to a lot of people?

Here, too, the answer is yes. There is not enough potable water. Billions of people on Earth will benefit from a good, cheap water purifier.

This makes the device so much more important than an invention that is beneficial to only a handful of people. And that's why it's worthwhile to work on it with lots of people.

3: Is the new technology affordable or accessible to many people?

It depends in this case. Water purifiers already exist, but they are expensive to make and use. They use a lot of energy, and you need quite a few to filter enough water for everyone who needs it. It's important that they become more affordable and energy efficient. Thankfully, Moore's law also applies to water purifiers. They are already better and more effective, and will continue to improve as scientists continue their work on the technology.[14] Most likely, there will be cheaper water purifiers for everyone within ten years.

The above example is about water purifiers, but you can use the test for any kind of invention. New environmentally friendly ways to generate power, for example. Medicine for common illnesses. Or a high-tech moisture-free mechanism for people who collect bellybutton lint. Would the first two inventions have a chance if you asked the three questions from above? What about the high-tech moisture-free bellybutton lint mechanism?

> CALCULATING YOUR CHANCES

Scientific American reported in 2011 that there are seven new ways to generate clean energy; these methods just weren't ready yet. And it was very uncertain whether they would ever work. On average, they had a 10 percent chance of working.[15]

You can easily calculate the probability that at least one of them will succeed:

Starting with your knowledge that one invention has 90 percent probability that it will fail, you can use Bayes' theorem to help you with the rest.[16] The probability that two inventions will fail is 0.9 times 0.9, and that is 81-percent probability. The probability that three inventions will fail is 0.9 times 0.9 times 0.9, and that is 73-percent probability. The probability that all seven inventions will fail is 0.9 times 0.9 times 0.9 times 0.9 times 0.9 times 0.9 times 0.9—a 48-percent probability! So there is a 52-percent probability that one of the inventions will succeed. In this way, you can literally calculate—somewhat—when we will use certain technologies.

Futurologists have different ways to research what will happen in the future, but no matter how good they are at it, they never know for sure. And the further you look ahead, the more uncertain it becomes. One thing is for sure: even in the future, we will need to eat and drink.

Hi!

We're about to eat dinner—I wonder what it is. It could be anything. French fries, of course. But maybe also pancakes, pizza, and hot dogs. What? Too unhealthy? Not anymore! There are all sorts of new ways now to make candy and junk food much healthier, but they taste just as good. Or maybe we won't be having junk food for dinner; maybe it will be something fancy, with all the bells and whistles. I do know dinner is in fifteen minutes, so my dad will start cooking soon.

5.
BREAD AND WATER

It doesn't take long to make dinner in 2030. Even the more complicated meals are ready in no time, thanks to smart cooking appliances. And there's almost no chance of anything going wrong. Why not? Keep reading . . .

A tasty hello from 2030!

> EATING DIFFERENTLY?

For hundreds of thousands of years, human beings only ate raw meat and plants. Once fire was wielded, food could be grilled over open fire, boiled in water, baked in ovens. Meals have been cooked in some fashion for tens of thousands of years since.

Just a few decades ago, the microwave came on the scene and radically changed our cooking ways. Will food and the ways we make it change even more in the next twenty years? Absolutely. In fact, what we eat and where we get it will change just as much. In 2030, there will be a billion more people on Earth than there are now—a billion people who all need to eat and drink. Will there be enough for everyone? That's an important question.

> THE PROBLEM OF RICHES

All these extra people are not the biggest problem. Even if there were three times as many, there might not be a problem necessarily. The problem is there will be millions more people living in wealthier countries, and that makes things tricky. There has been enough food for everyone on Earth for years, but it is distributed unevenly. Wealthier countries (such as the United States, Canada, Japan, and many European countries) import food from countries where huge numbers of people regularly go hungry or even starve. The farmers in the countries of Cote d'Ivoire, Brazil, Paraguay, Argentina, and Uzbekistan receive more money from exporting their produce than from feeding their fellow citizens. So these farmers grow cacoa, coffee, soybeans, corn, and cotton to sell to the richer countries instead of growing vegetables and grains for their own country.[1] There is a similar problem with water; there is often not enough potable water in poorer countries. Most of the water is used for the food and products that eventually go to the richer countries.[2]

HOW MUCH WATER DOES IT TAKE?

Nothing grows and lives without water. If you want to make food, you have to have water—to grow the crops, to feed the animal, and to process the food, from potato to potato chip, for instance. The amount of water needed to get the food from the field to your mouth depends on the product.

> A pound of potatoes = 35 gallons of water

> Small bag of potato chips = almost 8 gallons

> 1 apple = 33 gallons

> 1 glass of apple juice = about 60 gallons

> 5 ounces of vegetables = 10 gallons
  (to grow, harvest, and package)

> 1 slice of bread = almost 13 gallons

> 1 slice of cheese = about 38 gallons

> Half a pound of beef = 925 gallons[3]

> HUNGRY BECAUSE OF MEAT

It may sound strange, but meat is a big cause of hunger in the world. It mainly has to do with the lack of water. Wealthy countries usually have enough water, but big parts of the world are often too dry. The little water that is safe for drinking (potable) is used to make feed for the cattle in these richer countries. In the sidebar to the left you can see that it takes 925 gallons of water to grow half a pound of beef. It's less for other kinds of meat but still an awful lot. That is too much water for everyone to have meat. Americans are the biggest meat eaters in the world. They eat about two hundred pounds of meat per person per year. If everyone in the world ate that much meat, there would not be enough potable water—not for drinking, not for cattle, not for growing crops; not even if every drop was made available and used![4]

To feed all the cattle in the world, more than 1500 billion pounds of grain is transported per year. About one third of the feed for pigs and chickens comes from some of the poorest countries in the world. If you were to transport all this grain at once with one train, the length of the train would be six times the Earth's circumference.[5]

Another problem related to meat is that people need protein. Protein is an important nutrient our bodies need, and can be found in meat, grains, dairy, and legumes. Well, the proteins in meat have to come from somewhere: the cattle feed. It takes thirteen pounds of plant protein to create one pound of animal protein.[6] In poorer countries, people often have a protein deficiency because their nation's protein-rich products are exported to richer countries. These people become sick because of this deficiency—*very* sick in some cases.

> RICH PEOPLE IN OTHER COUNTRIES

In the previous century, the wealthiest areas were North America, Europe, and Japan. In the coming years, countries like China, India, and South Korea will be included. They are getting richer at a fast rate.

Soon there will be other wealthy countries too. Their people will also want coffee, cocoa, meat, cattle feed, and cotton. Moreover, a lot of crops are being cultivated to make biofuel. The richer the people, the more energy they need, and the more agricultural land is needed for biofuel. If there are tens of millions more rich people and hundreds of millions more poor people, there will definitely not be enough food for everyone in 2030—possibly sooner if nothing changes.[7]

WHERE DOES YOUR FOOD COME FROM?

Walk into your kitchen, take a look in the fridge and pantry, and read about where your food items come from. Usually "country of origin" is listed on the packaging in tiny letters. With coffee, chocolate, and fruit like bananas and pineapple, you don't even have to look. They come from faraway, tropical countries. Olive oil is often from the south of Europe—countries like Spain, Italy and Turkey.

Fish can be from anywhere in the world, but more often, it is imported from China.

Although the United States grows a tremendous amount of food, it imported 4.1 *billion* pounds of food from China in 2012 alone. In the winter, a lot of fresh fruits and vegetables come from Mexico, Central America, and South America.[8] And on and on. Researchers calculated how far an average meal of meat, potatoes, and vegetables has to travel before it ends up on our plates. The answer? All together, the ingredients traveled about 1500 miles.[9] That's the distance from San Francisco to Dallas—and that takes a lot of energy.

> EVERYONE TO THE CITY

There is something else going on with our food. Thousands of years ago, everyone grew their own food. This changed with the growth of cities and marketplaces. Even so, most people lived in the countryside, where they grew their own goods. In 2008, the world's population reached a new milestone, with more than half—3.3 billion—living in towns or cities. By 2030, that number is expected to reach 5 billion.[10] There isn't a lot of land among the shops, apartments, and offices, and there will be a smaller group of farmers working to feed a larger group of city folk. This won't make feeding everyone any easier.

In the past, there were lots of farmers growing different kinds of crops. Now, there are a lot fewer farmers, and they have large pieces of land on which they only grow one kind of crop. This makes the crops vulnerable to insects that eat produce. A plague of pests can cause an entire harvest to fail. So, farmers use poison, which is bad for the environment and our health; or they genetically modify the plants, a questionable method that some people believe is also bad for us.

Our food often comes from poor countries. And importing food at current levels could cause hunger and drought in the third world. Using pesticide and transporting the food across large distances damages the environment and is harmful to our health. And all of this will only get worse in the future.[11] Can we do something before then? Of course. There are lots of ideas that can contribute to the solution.

> THE FIELDS OF THE FUTURE

Who says an agricultural field has to take up a big piece of land? Who says an agricultural field has to be in the sun and rain all the time? And who says an agricultural field has to be outside? You might find the fields of the future in the middle of a city.

The field of the future is a tall, high-tech building with more floors underneath the ground. On every floor, different crops grow under special lamps. These lamps take very little energy and radiate exactly the right light that plants need to grow. The plants also get the best fertilizer, which makes them even better. (They grow so fast, by the way, that they have to be harvested several times a year.) The fields are water efficient, of course, and the buildings are sealed in such a way that water condensation is contained and reused. Rainwater supplements the condensation water, and poison and pesticides aren't needed because bugs can't get into the building. The best fruits and vegetables won't be coming from faraway countries anymore but from just down the hall or down the street.

Biofuel is made from the building's plant debris, which in turn produces heat for the entire building. Should there be a need for more energy, there is enough solar power to support the building as well as its crops. It's even possible that this field of the future will generate enough energy to send the excess to the homes around it.

These fields of the future aren't so futuristic anymore; they already exist and work really well. A 15,000-square-foot rooftop greenhouse in Brooklyn, New York, uses 5 percent of the land and just 1 percent of the water that a conventional farm uses to grow 100 tons of produce a year.[12] In a Vancouver (BC) downtown parking garage, a unique vertical farm of rotating stacked trays grows leafy greens on the rooftop—the first of its kind in North America. Harvests can't fail because of storms or droughts, and the harvest time is very exact.[13] Unfortunately, the fields of the future are just too expensive to build on a large scale at this time and do not make enough of a profit. It would take too many of these expensive buildings to feed the world, yet they still might solve a lot of problems in the future.

> VEGETARIAN BUTCHERS

Another way to lessen the food shortage problem is to eat less meat. You can do this by eating more beans, tofu, and cheese (or legumes, grains, and dairy), but people *love* their meat.

For decades, food that isn't meat but looks like meat has been available, but meat lovers everywhere often don't like those products. In a few years, there will be different meat alternatives on supermarket shelves and restaurant menus that taste so good that the biggest meat lovers won't be able to tell the difference between what's real and what's fake. You'll no longer have to kill a chicken, cow, or pig to have a barbecue. There are already products available that are hard to distinguish from the real thing,[14] but few people are buying and eating them. Not many know this, but a lot of meats are already supplemented with fake meat without anyone noticing.

NEW LIGHT ON FOOD

If you drive by greenhouses at night, you'll see how many lights are on. This takes an enormous amount of energy, yet plants do best under certain colors of light: a purple-blue and pinkish light. With energy-efficient lamps in that color, plants will do much better, and the greenhouses will only use 40 percent—or even less—of the energy than they used to.[15]

> FRANKENSTEIN FOOD

You've probably heard of Frankenstein's monster: a manlike being created by the scientist Victor Frankenstein in Mary Shelley's novel. This same name has been used when referring to a certain kind of food.[16] Scientists are creating new kinds of crops that grow faster and are less prone to disease or pests. They do this by taking genes from one organism and adding them to a plant's DNA. For instance, the genes that keep fish from freezing in cold water are added to the DNA of a strawberry seed to keep the fruit safe from frost. This technology is called "genetic modification," and the food that is made from these modified plants is called GM (genetically modified) or biotech food.[17] It sounds perfect, but some people worry that GM food will be monstrous—just like Frankenstein's creation—causing all sorts of problems. The crops could develop a new kind of disease, and they could be unhealthy for humans and animals. Scientists disagree with each other on this point, however, so in some countries, this way of producing food is allowed; in others, it is not.[18]

In the places where GM crops have been accepted, a lot of these crops have been cultivated. Up until now, this hasn't caused any major problems. In a few years, we'll know more about the pros and cons of this kind of food. Should there be more pros than cons, this GM food could help stop world hunger. And no one would call it Frankenstein food anymore.

FISHING FOR TROUBLE

As the world's population increases, there will be all sorts of shortages in energy, food, potable water, and valuable resources, but there is hope for all of these because governments and scientists are working toward alternatives and solutions. But for one shortage in particular, there is very little hope. If something isn't done soon, it will be too late.

There seems to be a strange competition taking place in the world: Who can build the biggest fishing boat? There is already a boat with a net that is a mile wide. You could easily fit twelve of the biggest airplanes into this net. But the winner is a Norwegian boat that catches almost a million pounds of fish every day and can store more than 15 million frozen fish.[19]

Together, all the boats in the world are harvesting three-fourths more fish than the oceans can sustainably provide. In addition to boats with nets, there are boats with fishing lines that run for miles. While you are reading this, a million fishhooks are floating in the water, baited with dead fish to catch the bigger fish (the Japanese fleet alone uses 100 million every year). Out of all the fish caught, up to 27 million tons of dead or almost dead fish go overboard each year because we don't eat them. Some 300,000 whales, dolphins, sea turtles, and porpoises die entangled in fishing nets. Over 100,000 albatross, seagulls, and other sea birds die every year because they get trapped in the fishing lines.[20]

If nothing changes, in little time, gigantic parts of the ocean will be empty of fish. The chances of this happening are great because not a single country does anything about this overfishing. In fact, most countries give their fishermen money to build bigger boats so that they can catch more fish. Not only fish will disappear; so will the birds that eat the fish and the coral that depends on the fish. There are already sections of the ocean that are empty, and fish have not returned to these areas. In 2030, millions of people will be starving because their most important source of food will have disappeared.[21]

Is there no hope? An invention that can bring the fish back? A better way of fishing? Fish-breeding machines? No. The only way to counteract this disaster is to out-law these destructive fishing practices. And that is not happening—not yet.

> HOW MUCH WATER GOES INTO YOUR JEANS?

Hunger isn't the only problem that will arise when there are more people on this planet. There is a huge shortage of water in the world; about 783 million people do not have enough clean water.[22] The shortage will only grow worse as temperatures rise. By 2030, it is estimated that human demand will exceed current supplies by 40 percent.[23] (We don't just use water to drink, shower, and flush the toilet; we use it to grow and make food.) And we need to account for the water needs of Earth's other inhabitants as well.

For a cup of coffee, you don't just need that little bit of tap water to make the coffee but another thirty-four gallons to grow and package the beans for that amount of coffee. There is very little that we can make without water. Even your laptop. You wouldn't know by looking at it, but the production process for just one laptop involves 2,800 gallons of water. And an average of 2,100 gallons is necessary to make a pair of jeans—to grow the cotton and to process it into the popular blue fabric— depending on where the cotton is produced.

(In India, for example, manufacturing the same amount of cotton requires almost 6,000 gallons of water.) In a lot of places, the current solution to finding more water now is to dig deeper wells, but this is a temporary solution. Exhausting natural wells will deplete water levels and eventually cause more drought.[24]

> FINALLY ENOUGH WATER?

Isn't it odd that there is a water shortage on a planet made up of two-thirds lakes, seas, and oceans? Only one percent of all that water is potable. So isn't it about time to make water purifiers that can turn seawater into drinking water? Water supply companies are working on it.

One of the most famous inventors in the world has been working to create a purifier like this for years. His name is Dean Kamen, and he has already invented a purifier that can make drinking water for one hundred people every day. The device is still very expensive to make and use, but Kamen expects that he can build these water purifiers for much less in a few years. Once this purifier or any of the others that are in development can start its work, the problem of potable water will, for the most part, be solved.[25]

> CORN SHRIMP, CRICKOS, AND BUGBURGERS

Would you like corn shrimp? Or crickos? And bugburgers? You would probably try them if they were prepared well. And chances are that you'll like them. But would you still want to if you knew they were grasshoppers, crickets, and insect burgers?[26] Maybe not. In parts of the world, it's very normal to eat bugs. In Asia and Central America, they are a delicacy. And they're good for you too. Most importantly, they could be a common source of protein in the future. They are much easier to raise than cows or pigs, and need less food and very little water.[27] Eating insects could be a *very* popular future food, but people have to want to try it first. There is some hope that insects will catch on as food: kids are usually more willing to try something new than their parents are.

> ROBOCOOKS

So our food will change. We'll eat different things and grow our crops another way. But our way of cooking will change significantly as well. Cooking can become as simple as receiving an email. How does that work? Like this:

A filmmaker in New Zealand makes a video, emails it, and you can watch it a few seconds later. A writer thinks of a story, puts it online, and you can read it from anywhere. A programmer in Japan creates a computer program, you download it, and start using it. A cook thinks of a recipe and sends that recipe to your oven. Huh? Well, if you can email videos, text, and computer programs, why not recipes? And why can't a recipe program an oven? All you need is an oven with a food processor that can be programmed and that can receive email. It wouldn't work for every dish but could for soups, pasta, stews, and dozens of meat and fish dishes. Now we just need a name for these future ovens. Robocooks? Kitchenbots? Eatomats?

In 2030, we'll spend less time in the kitchen than we do today. The average time people spend cooking decreases each year, and good kitchen appliances are a major reason. When the microwave and frozen meals came along, it coincided well with more and more moms working outside the home. A generation ago, around the time when your grandparents were raising your parents, women spent about two hours a day in the kitchen. Today, women have reduced their time to about an hour and seven minutes. (Interestingly, men have actually tripled their kitchen time since 1961 to more than half an hour a day, partly due to a cultural shift in gender roles. But advances in kitchen technology have helped to increase the desire to cook too.)[28] It will be even less if another new kitchen appliance is introduced. And what do we do with that extra time? Watch the cooking channel, of course.

> SUPERFOODS

Coffee helps you focus; that's why millions of people drink coffee in the morning. Warm milk helps you sleep. And did you know that fatty fish like salmon helps you remember things?

Food does more than fill your stomach; it can have an effect on your psyche and your mind. And we continue to learn about the substances that influence our performance. Food engineers are working on new drinks and foods all the time. We already have "smart" yogurt that helps you lose weight because it curbs your appetite, and oil and margarine that make your heart healthier. Food as medicine, in other words.[29]

In the future, there will be a lot more superfoods. Maybe even chocolate that makes you more creative, lemonade that makes you happier, or cookies that improve your eyesight.

> CANDY OF THE FUTURE

Kids love candy. But the problem is the sugar, which is bad for your teeth and can cause obesity. So in the future, will there be tasty, healthy candy without sugar? Definitely. There is already candy made from 100 percent fruit that tastes good and retains all the vitamins and fiber. But only a few people buy them; most still make unhealthy choices when they are in the candy aisle. The question is when will that change? In the past, childhood obesity was not the concern it is now. Since 1980, the number of obese children has almost tripled to about 17 percent of all American children and teenagers. If this increase continues, in 2030, more than half the children in the United States will be obese.[30]

Candy that You Can Breathe In

Obesity is very unhealthy, and candy makers know this. Maybe kids will be prevented from having candy in the same way that they are with alcohol and cigarettes. Willy Wonka will have to come up with new ideas so he can keep making candy! Like a flavor of candy that you can breathe in but doesn't have any of the calories and sugar. Or you'll have fruit that tastes like candy (there are already cotton candy grapes).[31] Imagine it: sweet, yummy candy that you can have more often because it is much better for you.

There will be more and more flavors and wacky combinations, like drinks that taste like pancakes, ice cream that tastes like potato chips, or peanut-butter-flavored marshmallows.[32] The improvements in savory snacks are developing at a faster rate. You can already buy chips and nuts in all kinds of flavors that have fewer calories than they once did. But that doesn't mean they are healthier!

Keep reading to find out how you'll stay healthy in 2030.

SKINNY PILLS

Our bodies are ingeniously put together; they're constructed like an amazingly smart bank. With your bank, when you have money left over, you put it in your account. And then you withdraw that money when you need it. In the meantime, it collects interest. Your body works just like that. If you eat more than you use, your body stores the food in the form of fat, which comes in handy when you don't have food and need energy.

In almost all of history, this is how we survived. Sometimes there was not enough to eat during the winter or a famine occurred, and sometimes harvests failed. Long live fat! It saved us. Yet now we live in a time when food is usually available, but our bodies still have the instinct to store fat. With "interest." And this hurts us more than it benefits us.

Scientists are working on a product that would turn off this mechanism in our bodies. If they succeed, you could use it to eat as much as you want, but your body would store less fat. So far, this product has worked for animals, and now they are testing it with humans.[33]

6.
SICK DAYS IN THE FUTURE? GOODBYE!

Hi!

I'm sick today. Just my luck. Nothing too bad; just a cold. We haven't gotten rid of these in 2030. Doctors say that's okay because it's normal to be sick and get some rest. But a lot of serious illnesses from your time can be cured now. We can even prevent some diseases, which is, of course, much better. You would think that there are more healthy people than in your time, but that's not the case. There are many more elderly people, and they aren't too fit anymore. On the other hand, there are people who think they will live forever. In short, there are plenty of changes happening!

A feeble hello from 2030!

> NO LONGER SICK?

If you want to stay healthy, you have to prevent getting sick. But if you do get sick, the doctor should see you as soon as possible in order to learn what is wrong with you. Then the doctor has to determine how to make you feel better, for which she needs the right tools. *All* these things will improve in the future.

> THE iMED

Let's cut to the chase: we will not be getting sick in 2030 as quickly as we are now. This is because of a little device that doesn't exist yet and doesn't even have a name. Let's call it the iMed. What is the iMed? Doctors have all sorts of apparatuses to measure your health. A heart rate monitor, a blood pressure gauge, a stethoscope, and blood sugar tests, for instance. The iMed is all these instruments and more. And you can read it yourself to see how healthy you are. Don't think that this means that you are hooked up to a machine all day, though. The iMed is a tiny chip in your body that you won't know is there. The chip sends information about your body to your computer or phone so you can see all your readings on a screen.

> CAN I TAKE THIS OR THAT?

The iMed immediately gives you advice on what to do when it's needed. It will tell you, for instance, that you need more exercise or more rest, or that you need to take in less salt or not eat any sugar. You can then decide whether you will or won't. If you're healthy, then you don't need to be meticulous about its advice, but you'll be fit for longer if you do. And if you are likely to get diabetes or heart disease, the iMed is very useful. A lot of people don't know what happens to their bodies when they eat unhealthily too often. They also have no idea about their current health. The iMed changes all of that. With the iMed, you'll always have a kind of personal doctor around to tell you how to stay healthy. If you think you can have that second piece of pie, the iMed will tell you if that is really the case, *and* it can send recipes for healthier alternatives instead.

> A NURSE IN YOUR BODY

Should something go wrong with your heart or you lose consciousness for whatever reason, the iMed will send an emergency signal to the closest real doctors. The doctors can immediately respond, but in some cases, the iMed can do what is needed. It can release medicine into your blood that will make you feel better immediately—just like getting a shot from a nurse. If you have diabetes, the iMed could regulate your insulin on its own. Another advantage of the iMed is that doctors will immediately have all the information they need about you if you have an accident or get sick. They'll see right away if you have allergies to certain medications or what illnesses and injuries you've had, which will make it much easier to treat you.

> THE HOSPITAL AT HOME

When you're sick now, you go to the doctor. And visiting the doctor's office takes time. The staff asks you questions, and checks your temperature, heart rate, and lungs, among other things—all things the iMed can do. You won't have to visit the doctor as often, and the doctor can spend more time looking for the cause of—and especially the solution to—your ailments. If your doctor can't figure it out, your information can be easily sent to a colleague who might know more, even if that colleague lives on the other side of the world. You'll get the best care that is out there, and it'll be similar to the care in hospitals. Thanks to all the new equipment, it will become easier to be treated from home, even by your friends and family. And wouldn't it be much nicer to recover in a known environment instead of in a cold, boring hospital room?

> WHEN WILL WE HAVE THE iMED?

The iMed will help keep people healthier, and diseases will be easier to trace and easier to cure. Cancer and heart disease are the most common illnesses from which people die. The sooner you detect either, the easier they are to treat. These new technologies will save a lot of lives.

Inventors like Raymond Kurzweil and Dean Kamen are working on devices like the iMed.[1] It will take years before they work well and even longer before they can be mass produced, but they have come a long way. In the meantime, other ways of preventing and curing diseases are being developed.

> THE BIG BREAKTHROUGH

Almost every month, there is an article in the newspaper about a breakthrough that will save hundreds of thousands of people in the future. For years, futurologists have predicted such a breakthrough for cancer. In reality, doctors and researchers are making progress at a very even pace. A real revolutionary improvement has yet to happen. Instead, doctors improve their patients' care. Fewer diseases are fatal, and if they are, the patients live longer than they used to—a gradual improvement that will continue. And yet, a really big improvement is still possible because, while the treatments are slowly getting better, medical knowledge is increasing at an enormous rate. In the last three years, we have found out more about cancer than in all of humanity's history, and this has to lead to improvement in treatment and cures. But when will this breakthrough happen? No one knows.

> A BODY THAT HEALS ITSELF

When you cut your finger, it bleeds. After a while, it stops bleeding, and a few weeks later, you can't even tell that you cut yourself. Your body *heals itself*—if it's healthy, at

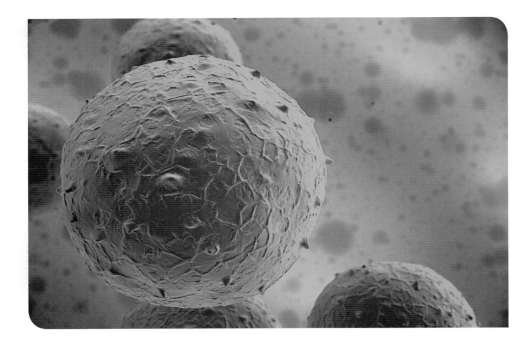

least. It's different for people who have certain illnesses, as the cells in their bodies can't do what they have to do. The cells are damaged, unable to repair themselves, but there is new hope.

At one time, you were made up of just two cells: a sperm cell and an egg cell. These cells joined, divided and grew, divided and grew, divided and grew . . . and so on. Some cells became bone, others an eye, and yet another, teeth. And it all took place on its own; you didn't have to do anything. The cells that are responsible for generating the tissues of your body are called stem cells. They are also responsible for a wound healing itself. Stem cells are cells that can become anything: skin, liver, bone—you name it. Regular cells can only be one thing—a skin cell, a liver cell, a bone cell—whatever they're programmed to be.

At this early stage, when a sperm cell and egg cell have joined, the resulting embryo is made up of only stem cells. The embryo becomes a fetus, and the fetus becomes a baby, who develops more regular cells as it grows. Children and adults are mostly made up of regular cells. Imagine if you could replace all the sick and damaged cells in your body with healthy stem cells so you could get better. You could regrow pieces of skin that are burned, generate new blood cells or even new kidneys, and cure an enormous number of illnesses. It's already being done and will be happening even more in the future.[2]

WILL YOU PRINT OUT A KIDNEY?

With a standard home or school printer, you can print a picture from the computer and hold on to it. The printer sprays ink on some paper, and you can see what it is. The paper has length and width, but what if you could spray the ink in layers so that the printout has height too? Not a little bit of height but high enough that this printing *up* starts to create an actual object? And what if you don't use ink but plastic? Then you have a 3-D printer—a printer that makes three-dimensional forms. You can print all sorts of shapes: a chair, a set of dentures, a mug. And just like pictures, an inventor in Tokyo can send the design to someone in Paris to print the item just moments later.[3]

With stem cells and 3-D printers, we'll be able to print complete organs. The stem cells will divide, and the printer will make sure they are in the right place. People with kidney disease can have a new kidney. In most cases of medical breakthroughs, it is only a question of when the technology will be ready to use. In the case of 3-D printers, we already know. Since 2008, we have been able to make new kidneys and other organs with them.[4] There are people walking around with bladders made by 3-D printers!

> ONLY GOOD NEWS?

It seems as if it will only get better in regard to our health. When it comes to medical knowledge and better medicine, this is true. At the same time, new diseases still threaten us— diseases so contagious that they can affect many victims in a short period of time. In previous centuries, there were diseases that became fatal and created widespread epidemics, or pandemics, like the bubonic plague. Though these diseases still exist, the epidemics no longer occur. Instead, more recently and in the future, dangerous flu epidemics take place. Between 1918 and 1920, tens of millions died from the Spanish flu; and in 2009, it was feared that it would happen again with the swine flu (also known as H1N1 virus). Fortunately, it wasn't nearly as bad in 2009 as it could have been.[5]

Because we can travel the world so easily, someone who has the flu can infect many other people very quickly. Someone

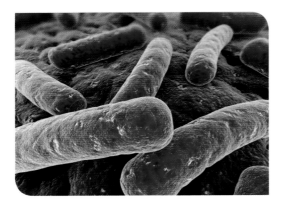

with a virus at an airport will be in contact with dozens of people from different countries who will then infect others as they travel and return home. Sometimes, deadly bacteria such as E. coli will turn up in our food, and there's no medicine against it. The chance for a big outbreak is *always* there, and the longer it takes for a big outbreak to take place, the longer scientists have to develop a way to counter it.

> OLD AND FIT

The older people become, the more likely they are to get sick (our immune systems age too). Since life expectancy is increasing, there will be more old people in the future, and some of them will be sick. But another trend is much more significant. Since we will be able to cure more illness, people won't just get older, they will also be fitter for longer. Right now, sixty-five-year-olds are as healthy as fifty-year-olds one hundred years ago.[6] In 2030, a seventy-five-year-old will be as fit as a fifty-year-old now. Can you imagine what being that old will be like? You'll still have to look before you cross the street, of course!

> CYBORGS

From 1974 to 1978, there was a popular TV show called *The Six Million Dollar Man*. The show was about an astronaut, Steve Austin, who was severely injured in the crash of an experimental spacecraft. Doctors patched him up but not in the usual way. He got an artificial eye, a mechanical arm, and two mechanical legs. And his artificial limbs did not make him disabled but *stronger* than everyone else. Everyone who watched the show knew that this wasn't possible; in the distant future maybe. Well, guess what? That distant future is *now*.

We know of pirates with a hook, soldiers with a wooden leg, and even ancient Romans using ivory for dentures. It's nothing new to replace parts of your body if they don't work or if they are missing. For years, doctors did nothing more than try to replace the missing part with something that was close to it. There are plastic hands and glass eyes that look

FINGERS ON YOUR CHEST

When you move your arm, you send signals from your brain to the nerves that then move the muscles. Similarly, those nerves send a signal to your brain when you feel something—if you were to touch stinging nettles, for instance. Yet if you don't have an arm, then you don't have any nerves. So how do you move a mechanical arm?

If someone loses their entire arm in an accident, the nerves usually end at the shoulder, and the signals from the brain will also end there. If someone without an arm acts like he does have an arm, the signal won't go beyond the shoulder unless the doctors have moved the nerve endings to muscles that will react, perhaps to the pectorals. The pectoral muscles will then send a signal to the artificial arm. They will tell the arm to stretch or contract, for instance, and the mechanical arm will follow these commands. The artificial fingers can also *feel*. With sensors at the fingertips, they can feel the pressure when the hand touches or holds something. Then these sensors send that information to the nerves that send it to the brain.[7]

Complicated? You bet. Thankfully there have been successful experiments with sending signals directly to the brain so that you can operate your new hands with your brain instead of your pectoral muscles.

like the real thing, but they can't move. Right now, there are artificial arms that do move. You can pick ripe tomatoes without crushing them; you can pick up a bottle of water and put it to your lips; you can even scratch your nose. There are artificial legs that people can walk on, run on, play basketball on. There are even artificial eyes with which people with a certain kind of blindness can see again.[8] And that is only the beginning.

> BONES ON THE OUTSIDE

With human beings, the skeleton is on the inside. Our muscles wrap around the bones, and it's all covered with skin. With

snails, the skeleton is on the outside, and that can have its advantages. The snail can live in its skeleton and crawl out of it—something people can't do. And having a skeleton on the outside allows the addition of extra muscles, which is exactly what some scientists are working on now. They have made an exoskeleton with mechanical muscles (called a "powered exoskeleton") with which soldiers can carry more than two hundred pounds for hours.[9] Then, when they're done with their assignment, they simply take off the skeleton.

This technology also helps those people who have trouble moving their arms and legs. The exoskeleton feels whatever movement the muscles want to make and gives them the extra power to do so. Disabled people can do everything again—and more. By the time you are eighty years old, this technology will be so advanced, who knows how proficient and fast a person could walk![10] With all these new technologies, we will be able to replace and improve every muscle and body part.

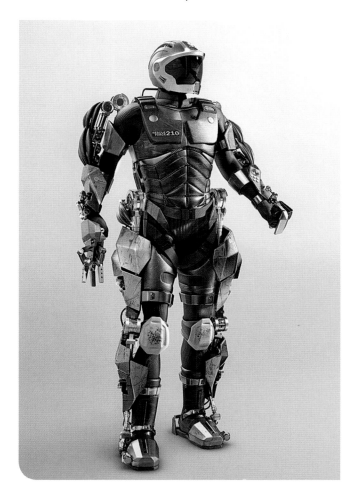

> LIVE FOREVER?

Is it possible that people will live forever? Some say yes. You can't avoid accidents, of course, but if you avoid taking big risks, then (according to some people) you can become very old. One way that we can become immortal has to do with a protein called "telomerase."

As we get older, our cells stop dividing, our muscles and bones become brittle, our skin loses elasticity, and our bodies start getting sick. Telomerase is a substance that counteracts this deterioration. It is a protein that causes cells to keep dividing properly so that we remain like new. Forever young, in other words. In experiments with this protein, mice lived up to fifty percent longer.[11] If people can become as old as 100 years today, they will become 150 years old with this substance. Telomerase sounds like a miracle drug, but it has a major disadvantage: it increases the chance of developing cancer, which is very dangerous. There is plenty of room for improvement, though, as scientists have only been working on this for the past few years. Will they be successful in stopping the body's aging process? We'll know more by 2030.

Another way to live forever would be to keep the head—the main "computer"—but replace one's body with artificial legs, arms, and a torso. You'd still exist and think but, for the most part, be a robot. Speaking of robots, what will they be like in the future?

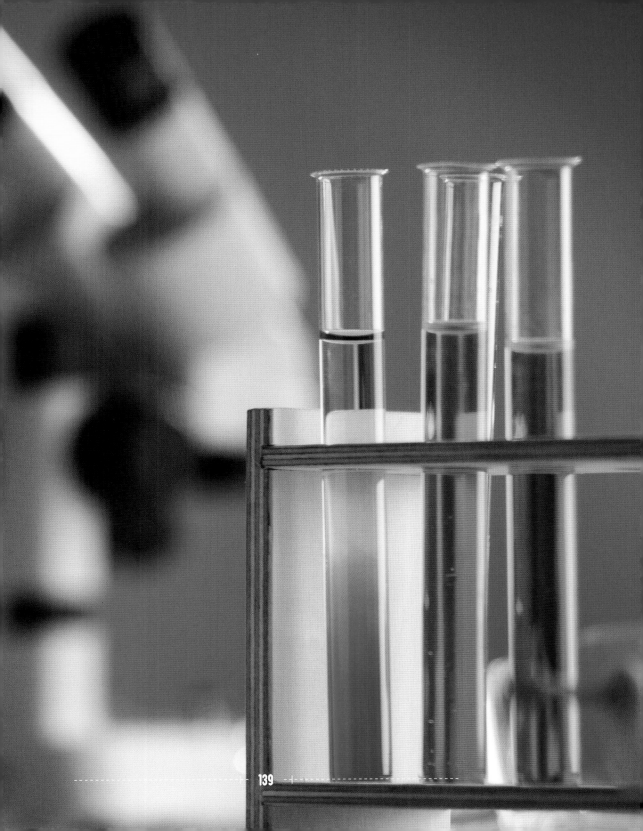

7.
THE AGE OF THE ROBOT?

Hi!

Can you think of devices that were different when you were little? I'm sure you can. Computers couldn't do as much and were a lot slower. They were also much bigger. Mobile phones were only used to make phone calls and send text messages. Most television sets were super heavy. And how often would you see GPS navigation in a car? A lot changed in a few years, didn't it? You can imagine how different it is in 2030. In the next ten years (according to Moore's law—remember?), a lot more will change than in the last ten years. How cool would it be if you could time travel to see my world? While we can do a lot in the future, we can't time travel . . . yet!

An ultramodern hello from 2030!

> SPACE TRAVEL AND FLYING CARS

When you look at older books about the future, you see a lot of the same ideas: robots, flying cars, and travels to distant planets. These subjects were really popular. Take space travel.

When Will We Go to Mars?

In the early days of space exploration, launching a rocket was the kind of news that everyone talked about for days, especially if it was a rocket to the moon or other unique destinations. Space exploration was very exciting and important—and still is (even if rocket launches are more common these days). Without astronautics, we would not have the high-tech mobile phones or personal computers that we have now. It wouldn't be as easy to keep up to date with news from around the world, and we wouldn't have navigation in cars either. All these technologies derive from the telecommunications first used by NASA. And tech like navigation systems and cell phones rely on the 200 or so satellites that orbit Earth, sending signals from one side of the world to the other.[1] Thanks to the satellites and space stations in orbit, scientists can also see how our planet is doing. There is much more knowledge about climate change and other environmental issues.

Futurologists in the past predicted trips to Mars and other planets by now. They expected that people would inhabit a colony on the moon, and they thought that regular people (not just astronauts) would travel through space. This last prediction is somewhat true these days; you just have to be very rich to be a space tourist.[2] And there is certainly more to be discovered and studied about Mars, life on other planets, the origin of Earth and the universe, and so on. But why would we travel to Mars? Why go and live on the moon? A lot can go wrong during this kind of mission, and it costs billions of dollars that could perhaps be better spent on fighting poverty and hunger, providing education and healthcare, or solving environmental issues.

Space exploration is interesting and important, but the world's governments are only investing a small portion of their budgets toward it.[3] There will most likely be another exciting new era of space travel and discovery like the sixties and seventies of the last century, just not before 2030—unless space tourists are willing to pay the bill.

Flying Cars

The space-travel story is a similar one for flying cars; it's possible, and there are experimental cars that can fly, but they are really more plane than car, and are still expensive

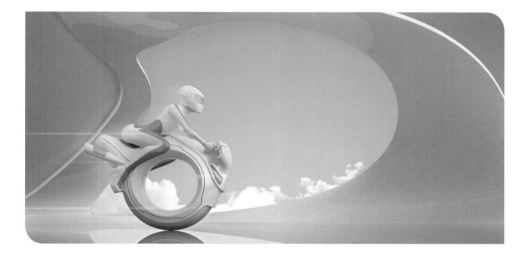

and dangerous.[4] To fly, you need a pilot license and, more importantly, permission to enter airspace so that you aren't interrupting air traffic and endangering the planes that are already in the sky. It's not easy to get that permission, so there's not much you can do with a Ford Flyer, Mercedes Boeingz, Volkswagencopter, or Jet Jaguar. Perhaps, in the distant future, there will be flying cars, when air traffic is safely monitored by robots and computers, but that won't be for quite a while. Cars will still go through many changes, but in very different ways.

> GAS PUMP OR ELECTRICAL OUTLET?

In the coming years, cars will be lighter, cleaner, more energy efficient and more aerodynamic than they are now. Even if you drive every day, you'll only need to gas up once a week. And there will no longer be any noise pollution; cars will be as quiet as mice. In ten years or so, they will *really* be different. Not so much their shape but in terms of their technology.

Car manufacturers are working on all sorts of new cars, but there are two popular models among them: one is the electric car and the other is a car that runs on hydrogen gas in the form of a "fuel cell." Both have their pros and cons.[5] They are both better for the environment because they don't emit carbon dioxide, a leading cause of global warming. Electric cars, however, need their batteries charged, and that

can take some time. So, it's not yet possible to take an electric car very far, because the battery will run out. Hydrogen fuel cells don't have that problem, and hydrogen gas works just like gasoline but a lot more efficiently. Gassing up is quick, and the car goes far. The only problem is that it takes a lot of energy to make hydrogen gas.[6] Depending on how the hydrogen gas is produced, a hydrogen-fuel-cell car ultimately requires more energy than an electric one.

> SMARTER CARS

A hybrid car combines technologies, using a fuel-like alcohol or gasoline when its battery is low. This allows the car to utilize a more efficient, environmentally friendly source of energy without running the risk of running out of power and being stranded. Another option is to replace the car battery instead of charging it. Then, when you drive off with your new battery, the old one is recharged and sold to the next driver who needs it. Though this alternative sounds great, it only works if all electric cars use the same batteries or if swapping stations carry all kinds of batteries.[7]

This is the challenge for both electric and hydrogen-fuel-cell cars: any new car technology won't take hold unless it's used in more places by more people. Having a hydrogen-fuel-cell car doesn't make sense unless you can gas up anywhere and everywhere. But there are few hydrogen gas stations because there aren't many hydrogen-fuel-cell cars, and those cars won't be used until there are gas stations that they can use; the two scenarios are dependent on each other. Fortunately, the majority of car manufacturers are planning to use these new technologies, which means the gas stations and drivers will eventually follow.

In a few years, the biggest problems with these models will be solved, but one problem remains: Where will we get the energy to produce the electricity and hydrogen? If we keep generating that energy from fossil fuels like coal, the cars will still not be good for the environment!

> MY CAR IS KEEPING AN EYE ON YOUR CAR . . .

Electric or hydrogen fuel cell, a car continues being a driving vehicle that takes you from one place to another. It's interesting to look at how the car of the future will be doing that. More safely to be sure.

A driver isn't paying attention and doesn't see in time that the car in front of him is braking. *Boom!* A driver forgets to use her turn signal when leaving the freeway, and the car behind her doesn't know that she's changing lanes. *Boom!* A driver doesn't have his lights on in the fog, and the car behind him doesn't see him in time. *Boom!* All these collisions won't be happening in the near future. Cars will recognize each other. They will know where other cars are driving, and they will know their direction and speed. They will be able to respond immediately if a car in front of them brakes—and do so much faster than any human could.

Just like locator apps on a phone can tell you where your friends are, technology in cars will work similarly. Cars will have sensors and transmitters so that they can communicate with each other. ("Be careful. I'm twenty yards in front of you and braking suddenly.") With this technology, you can no longer drive through a red light; the car gets similar transmissions from traffic lights so that it knows when the light will change. And the car can anticipate the traffic situation so a lot fewer accidents take place. Smart cars like these are in development, and it won't be long before they are on the road, intervening at critical times.[8]

THE ROAD OF THE FUTURE

The car of the future is an exciting subject, but so is the road of the future. A good road can help save energy and prevent accidents.

Nobody likes to live close to a freeway because of the smell and the noise. Fortunately, roads are being made that are quieter than those we have

now. If the cars become electric, you'll barely hear anything; and the exhaust gases will have disappeared too. The road of the future will be made of solar panels that generate power for electric road markings, traffic lights, and nearby homes and businesses. The panels can also heat the road to keep off snow and ice.[9] And even more spectacularly, they will repair themselves. Should the road rip or tear, it will release little nodules. These nodules will burst open and release oil that hardens into new road material. The rip is immediately filled, and the road lasts longer.[10]

> AUTOPILOT CARS

If a car can intervene at critical moments, why can't they drive themselves? Actually, they *can*. For years now. In 1995, there was a car that drove itself from Munich, Germany, to Copenhagen, Denmark. It passed other cars and stopped for pedestrians at the crosswalk. And only in a few cases (5 percent of the entire trip) did the human driver have to take control.[11] But that was more than fifteen years ago . . .

There are already buses that take passengers to their destination without a driver. In 2010, four autopilot vans drove from Italy to China, about 8,000 miles. The drivers still had to take control a few times, but they arrived on time, without a scratch.[12] When can we expect to see an autopilot car on the road? When can we "drive" one? In 2006, experts thought it wouldn't be until 2056 that we would see them on the road. Two years later, the technology had improved enough that they thought it would happen by 2020.[13] There is one company that says it's already possible, however. A company everyone knows for something very different: Google.

> FIND MY HOUSE

Google is known as the very popular internet search engine, but they do a lot more. Google buys the patents of many inventions and uses those to make things like the autopilot car,[14] which works perfectly.

Altogether, the driverless Google cars have driven over 150,000 miles without any problems, crossing busy freeways, taking tricky turns, and squeezing through small, busy streets. These autonomous cars do so well, they are faster and better on an obstacle course than human drivers. Google's objective is not to make a car as safe as when a person drives one but safer—*a lot* safer. These cars could prevent hundreds of thousand of accidents each year.[15]

The only problem is that, so far, few states and few countries allow people to ride in a car without a driver. But it shouldn't be long before that changes. Maybe the first driverless cars will be on your street as soon as 2016. Except . . .

What is driving the car? Is there a robot in the driver's seat? No. Cameras and lasers scan the environment and superfast computers send the steering, acceleration, and brake commands to the car. There is no need for a robot.[16]

But what about those robots? Where will they be needed? Will there be any robots at all? Of course. They are already here.

> WHAT IS A ROBOT?

Most people think of those funny, stiff figures when they think of robots. Those robots have been around for decades, mostly

as toys. People used to think that robots like these would be doing household chores for us, like washing the dishes. Isn't a dishwasher easier? Well, could they do the laundry? No, the washing machine does the laundry. Cook for us? No, because faster-and-easier-than-microwave meals don't exist. And lots of other appliances work with a remote. So what could we use a robot for?

Lots of different things. In fact, there are lots of robots that are already being used; they just don't look like funny little stiff people. You probably wouldn't identify them as robots, but robotlike machines make most cars, televisions, and other appli-

ances; many factories can't do without them. In car factories, the robots put the cars together, fasten the parts, and paint the metal exterior. Not a single human being is involved.[17]

There are many more robots that do different things, like robot snakes that can crawl into the rubble of a collapsed building to look for survivors. Or little robots that can cross difficult terrains with a camera; they would go into a radioactive area, for instance, to examine the defective reactor plant. There are robots that do really dirty work, like patrolling sewers. And there are plenty that come in handy in everyday life. For years, small solar-powered, self-propelling robots have been mowing thousands of lawns. And there are the vacuum bots that look very similar.

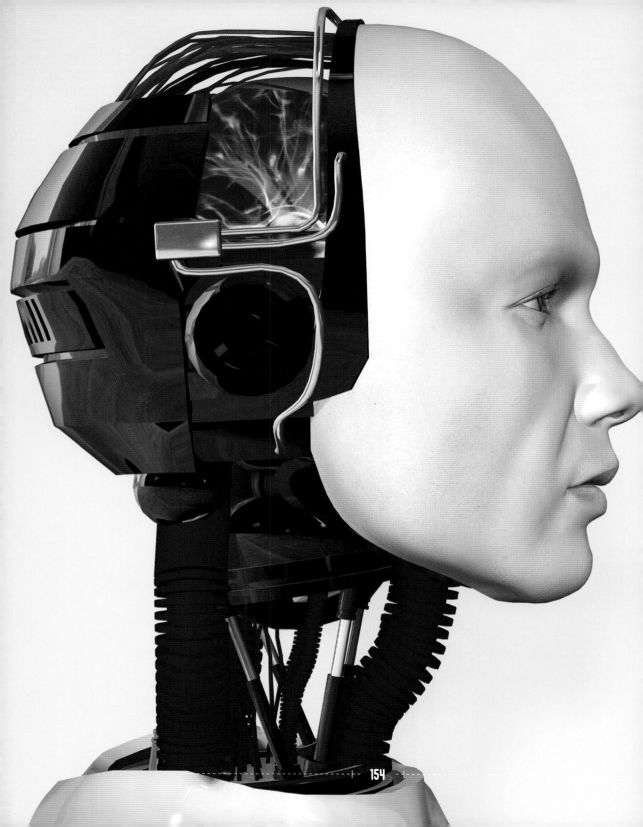

They move around in circles, vacuuming everything they find. In short, the future of robots is already here.[18] They will become even more impressive, however, and we'll start to see it in the next few years.

> THE ROBOTS OF TOMORROW

All the above-mentioned robots can do just one thing. There is no point in talking to them like they are people or animals because they don't listen or follow your instructions. For some time, however, robots that do react to our voices and bodies have been in development. They'll look at and listen to us, then do something or answer our questions. But these kinds of robots are very complex. They have to understand our voices, say something back, and make sense; they have to be mechanically perfect. If we look at something, they have to figure out what we are looking at and then look at it themselves. Then they have to use their robot hands, feet, and arms to do what we asked.[19] This kind of robot will exist.

> JACKS OF ALL TRADES

On the next page, you will see Professor Henrik Scharfe. He re-created himself as a robot; you have to look twice to see who is

who. The robot has the same facial expressions. He even blinks his eyes and appears to be breathing. What else can he do? Not much.[20]

Even though a team of scientists has been working on the robot for years, he can't walk or talk on his own; his speech and movements are meticulously programmed. It's that difficult to make a good humanoid robot. But the day will come when this robot can do more, like move around like a human, and listen and talk back.[21]

There are robots that are really good at other things. Robots that can climb stairs. There are soccer robots. Robots with which you can play table tennis. Robots that play the piano. If you put all that technology in one robot, you'll have a superrobot that can do everything.

As great as that sounds, we're not there yet. Even if you've never played soccer or table tennis, chances are you will beat the robot. But a start has been made and developments are speeding up, especially because there are more and more robots who can do different things. Then one robot designer can learn from another robot designer and stack the inventions to create a new, better robot.

ROBOSOLDIERS THAT EAT

What about a robot that can scan a large area for weapons and enemies? One that reacts faster than a human and is stronger too? A robot like that would come in handy in the armed forces. You could send it to the most dangerous areas. And the loss of a robot is considerably less than the loss of a human life. Fortunately, robots for warfare are already in development and use.

There aren't too many yet, but it would make sense that these kinds of robots would be very useful in future wars and conflicts. They don't get tired and need very little to keep going. And you can make them very small. Losing power, whether batteries or fuel, is one potential problem, but a solution exists already. There is a military robot that works on an engine that needs fuel. The robot knows how to look for and get this fuel from certain plants and flammable materials that are in its surroundings. It feeds itself, in other words.[22]

> HUMAN OR ROBOT?

Do you ever chat online? How do you know that you are chatting with a person, not a robot? At this time, this question is unnecessary. There are programs that pretend to be human, but you can usually tell within a few lines of chatting. The program has to be unbelievably smart and complex to pull it off. It has to understand everything that you are writing, respond without mistakes, and react like a person. This is not possible yet, but it's just a matter of time. There are already a few programs that have fooled some people. Once it does work, you can put the program into a talking robot, and you'll have a robot that talks and sounds like a real friend.

> THE SMARTEST ROBOT

Computers have been beating people in chess since 1997.[23] This is also the case with other strategic and trivia games. There is also a computer, named Watson (after the IBM CEO in chapter 4), who can play Jeopardy!

In Jeopardy! the rules are that you have to answer the question in the form of a question. For instance, if the question is "What is the capital of France?" then

the answer is "What is Paris?" The questions are much harder than this, of course, and can include riddles, puzzles, and word games.

In 2010, Watson played against two people on the show. Watson had to understand the question, think of the answer, turn it into a question, and say it clearly through a speech program. And guess what? Watson won! That's how smart Watson was in 2010.[24] Since then, he has been put to work for IBM clients. By drawing from an unlimited database and learning from his interactions with people, the supercomputer is better at customer service than people. He could even improve patient care by accessing and cross-referencing the patient's records with the latest studies and data, and best treatment options.[25] Put a computer like that in a superrobot that can do everything *and* looks human, and you have the robot of the future.

With Watson, you can see what computers are good at: getting facts out of books and encyclopedias and making calculations. They're better than anyone with facts and numbers. Yet they have their weaknesses. They can't be resourceful or creative in finding solutions—not yet anyway. The question is whether they will by 2030. Until they can think independently, they can help us think of creative solutions in the meantime.

> YOUR ROBOT IN THE FUTURE

The question is not whether we will have a robot at home but *when*. And what will you do with it? It'll be lots of fun to have around. People have had robots for years that do less, but they still had fun with them. It will get a lot more interesting when you can talk to your robot or play tennis with it. If your sister doesn't want to play, you can play with your robot. But these robots won't just be there as toys.

For the elderly or disabled, a robot can be useful around the house. It can help with getting out of bed, offer support when walking, and do all sorts of household chores.

It wouldn't be an unnecessary luxury. Right now, there are more working people than older people, but that will change.

The number of elderly people will increase, and there will be fewer people between the ages of twenty and sixty-five to do the work that needs to be done. It'll be good to have robots take over some jobs. Robots in 2030 could work at a front desk in a hotel or at places that need an information booth, like tourist attractions and train stations.

Robots can do dangerous work, like cleaning skyscraper windows, fighting fires, and tending to leaking nuclear power plants. They make safer drivers of buses, trains, and trucks than humans. And they'll do "boring" work, like making sure people don't misbehave in museums, and handling the night watch or security at a hospital and other places where not much happens. They can also do work in places that are difficult for humans to get to—high in the atmosphere or deep in the ocean, for example.

> NANOBOTS

Robots won't just become better and smarter; they will become smaller—*much* smaller. Currently, there are robots that are so small you can't see them with the naked eye. These "nanobots" don't look like the robots in movies and books, but they can do what other robots do: perform tasks on their own. Scientists are working on nanobots that can look for cancer cells in our bodies and destroy the cells when they find them. This way, cancer can be cured without the miserable and troublesome treatments that we have now. The first trials ridding humans of cancer cells were successful, and a rat has been cured of diabetes with nanobots.[26]

> OTHER FUTURE GADGETS?

Have you ever watched old television shows? Think about the technology that was present at that time these shows were made. Lots has changed, especially in the last twenty years. Most people didn't have mobile phones, or if they did, they were as big as a carton of milk. The internet was useless; and if you wanted to send a message to your cousin overseas, you mailed a letter, which arrived two weeks later. We can't know for sure what technological advances will happen in the next twenty years, but another invention like the internet could change *everything*. There are some new technologies we do know about, however, because they will be available soon.

> TRANSLATOR GLASSES

Translating programs on the internet let you translate dozens of languages to English in seconds. And while some mistakes may occur in the translation, you can still understand what the

text is about. Likewise, for the deaf and hard of hearing, there is closed captioning for movies and television shows, which is usually a fairly accurate translator. Viewers read what is being said just like they would read subtitles for foreign films. And you know what? Computers primarily provide the closed captioning; few humans actually work on them.

When you have a program transform what is said into text that you can read, you could have that text translated almost instantly by one of the translating programs. Put that text on the bottom of a pair of glasses, and you'll have live subtitles for *any* language. You won't have to learn to speak French to understand the baker in Paris. And if the baker has a pair of the glasses too, then you can just respond in English. But no worries if he doesn't have them. Just turn the translation around, and the glasses will translate what you said in English. Or let the baker borrow your glasses . . .

> INVISIBILITY SUIT

Some things like time travel and eternal life won't happen until far into the future. The question is whether we'll ever have all the knowledge to accomplish these things. Just never say never, because lots of people thought flying and going to the moon would never happen. A suit that would make you invisible sounds like the same kind of fantastic unreality. Yet that technology is more possible than you would think. Researchers have successfully performed a few experiments that lead them to believe that an invisibility cloak will one day be possible.[27]

How does it work? Think of a stone that you're holding under running water. The water hits the stone, then envelopes the stone, and then returns to its original shape under the stone. The stream of water above and under the stone looks exactly the same, and scientists have found a way to use light to do the same thing. Imagine a friend is thirty yards away from you and there is a car between you. The car has an invisibility cloak that bends the light around it like the water around the stone, making it invisible to your eye.[28] Complicated? You bet! You can't count on cheating at hide-and-go-seek anytime soon, but your children might when they are about ten years old.

> BRAIN COMPUTERS

A long time ago, people understood very little about the brain. Ancient Egyptians even believed that we thought with our hearts and that the brain wasn't all that important.[29] These days, however, more and more is known about the brain. It's known which parts of the brain are responsible for certain tasks and behaviors, and what the brain does when we are thinking of particular things.

Are you using your imagination? A very small part of your brain becomes highly active when you do. Are you trying to remember something? There is another part for that.

Scientists have learned so much about the brain that they've found a way to make some deaf people hear again and some blind people see again. And they've applied electronic devices to parts of the brain to treat serious afflictions like epilepsy, Parkinson's disease, and OCD (obsessive-compulsive disorder). This technology, called "deep brain stimulation," is a form of "neuromodulation" (which has been around since the 1960s),[30] and it could be the beginning of having computers attached to our brains so we can improve how we think and remember. It may sound dangerous—and it is—but it will be a while before the first person is attached to a brain computer. Possibly by 2030.

> EVERYTHING MAKER

Everything around you is made up of molecules. This book, the table, the Himalayas, the sun, the moon and stars, and *you*. A sugar cube, for instance, is made up of carbon dioxide, hydrogen, and oxygen molecules. In the chapter about health and sickness, you learned about the 3-D printer, a printer that can build any object. Imagine you had a molecule printer—a 3-D printer that let's you build an object molecule by molecule. You could make anything you wanted! You'd simply find out what molecules something is made of—the molecules of a steak, mobile phone, battery—and then send that data to the printer. The printer is hooked up to tubes with the raw materials it needs to make different molecules, and with those, it prints what you wanted, layer by layer. At home, you'll have a small printer to print toys, gadgets, phones; and if you have a larger space and printer, you can print a car or a whole kitchen—in *hours*, not days!

Will this new technology really exist? According to some experts, yes; they think we'll be using it in ten to forty years. Others say it won't happen for another hundred years because it's too complicated. No matter how long it takes, it's being worked on by many scientists who believe it *will* be a reality one day. And when it is, we will be able to make *anything* we want, changing the world in unimaginable ways like technologies of the past—all over again.

ONE LAST THING...

Remember the first words of this book? "Do you want to laugh? Read this book in 2030! It's full of predictions for the future, and chances are that they are completely wrong." Of all the predictions in this book, this is the most likely to come true.

It is always funny to read old books about the future. When you do, you'll notice one thing: we can do *more* than what people predict, and that is certainly the case for what you've read here. The chances are great that the technology of 2030 is much more advanced than this book predicts. What kind of machines and tools will we have? No idea. In 1900, no one thought about computers and the internet; no one could have come up with it. But look at how important they are now! Or think about phones that take a picture that you can send around the world in seconds. Or 3-D printers. Even with the largest imagination, you could not have imagined a hundred years ago how we live now.

So when you think about the future, your imagination cannot be big enough. Maybe you should spend some time thinking about it, and then write down your ideas and predictions. Keep your notes and read them again in 2030. Are they right? Then you should definitely write a book about the future!

See you in 2030!

EXERCISES IN FUTUROLOGY

You may wish to have a notebook and pen on hand for this section of the book—so you can keep track of all your ideas and predictions. And who knows? Maybe one of them will come true, and then your notebook will appear in a museum to famous futurologists one day!

> WHY SHOULD YOU BOTHER READING THIS BOOK?

So there are wild cards and bad-luck cards that determine our future. The most important wild card is probably the intelligence of computers. Computers can already do math and remember more than we ever could, but they are still not capable of having creative thoughts and ideas on their own; people program everything a computer "thinks." Yet some experts predict that it is only a matter of time before computers will start to think of creative solutions for hard-to-solve problems—solutions that are better and smarter than any human being could come up with.

With the help of independently minded supercomputers, we could build even better computers, which could then build even better computers, and then those would build . . . Well, you know, and so on and so on. We'll eventually have computers that are infinitely smarter than us and can help us solve lots of problems. Think about a world with thousands of times more knowledge and intelligence than we have now. What would that world be like?

Try to imagine what it would be like if those kinds of computers existed. Would you rather have your country governed by "stupid" human politicians or by superintelligent computers? If you were sick, would you rather get advice from a supercomputer or from a human doctor that makes human mistakes? And wouldn't it be better if computers did scientific research rather than humans, with their limited brains?

If these computers exist, what would people do? Especially if, by that time, robots could perform all our physical work better and faster than us. What would we do to keep ourselves busy? Will we have vacation all the time, leaving the computers and robots to do our work? Would humans ever want to give up making decisions and leave it to the computers? Would you want that?

In some science-fiction books, computers and robots take over the world. Is it possible, do you think? Or would we never let it get that far? Would a computer ever have reasons to take power? Why would it do that? Or are we unable to answer that question because we don't think like a supercomputer?

> TECHNOLOGY EVERYWHERE

Imagine computers and computer chips so small and cheap that you can truly put them in *anything*. You could have a bicycle that corrects you when you make a mistake that could cause you to fall. Or that prevents you from crashing into something. Or that calculates which gear is best. What else could you do with all that technology on your bike?

A flowerpot with a computer could indicate when a plant needs water. A lamp could calculate how much light is needed in a room and determine how bright to shine. A window can darken if too much light is coming through on a warm and sunny day. Your faucet could warn you if the water is so hot that it will burn you. Look around you at all the appliances and objects in your life. What could you do with them if you added a computer?

And outside? What could you do with computers inside streetlights, garden fences, swings, bridges, and traffic signs? What would be the advantage? Perhaps by answering these questions, you've already thought of something that we could use in the future!

> 1. A TOUR OF YOUR NEW HOME

If you could decorate your walls at home with electronic paper, what would the walls look like? Close your eyes and imagine the ideal room (everything you can think of can be in it!). What would that room be like? What else can you think of that would make your room nice, comfortable, fun, and exciting?

And what seems better to you: a house built with natural materials that are sustainable and green? A house built with synthetic materials that offer all sorts of advantages due to their technology? Or maybe both?

Maybe homes in the future will be built with a material like clay that you can shape into all sorts of models. What else can you think of for the house of the future? Is it still in danger of fire or will it be completely inflammable? Would you still need to paint it or would it change color on its own?

How can today's homes be improved? By answering this question, you'll get closer to the home of the future. Because one thing is for sure: our homes will be better, more comfortable, and safer.

> 2. SPACESHIP EARTH

There is a lot of money to be made with oil and gas. An unimaginable amount of money. Some of the richest people and businesses make their money with oil and gas. Some countries became very wealthy because of oil and gas. But at some point in the future, oil will run out. What do you think will happen to all those countries, companies, and people? Will they look for other ways of making money before the wells run dry? What would you do if you earned your income with oil and gas?

What choice would you make in the case of "spaceship Earth"? Would you listen to the ninety-five doctors who say that you are sick—even though they don't all agree on what's wrong with you? Would you take radical measures or would you wait and see? How do you think it will be with the world when its citizens can no longer deny the diseased state of the Earth?

Moore's law also applies to clean energy. Compare it to the first computers. You can compare the solar panels and wind turbines that we currently have with the computers we had decades ago. The more research we do, the easier and cheaper it will be to get and use clean energy. Imagine clean energy having the same increase in progress as the speed and memory of computers. Clean energy will eventually be very cheap. Now imagine that energy is completely clean and costs nearly nothing. What could be possible? Flying, for example, is very expensive because of fuel, but that will no longer be the case. Transportation will become very cheap. The production of materials takes a lot of energy, so the products made from those materials will be cheaper.

What will happen when travel becomes very cheap? Will we go everywhere all the time? And if all our things and products become cheaper, will we buy more? Or not so much?

> 3. FROM DIRTY HUMAN TO "GREEN" AS AN ANT

What can you think of to rid us of the plastic soup in the oceans? Dispatch robot ships that collect all the plastic? Develop a kind of bacteria that eat plastic? Invent a plastic magnet that attracts all the plastic bits in the water? Or do you have another idea?

Cleaning up the world's oceans is only part of the solution. Because every day, there is more and more plastic added to the heap. Even if only one in a thousand people littered plastic, millions of people would still be polluting the Earth. And in reality, there are actually a *lot* more people who throw their trash into the streets. It's better to simply stop making things from plastic; then we wouldn't have this problem.

What is made of biodegradable plastic in your house? Look around you and in the cupboards. Would it make a difference if all the plastic things in your home were made of different materials? What about everything on your whole street? Your whole town? Your whole country?

Do you think people will ever make everything Cradle to Cradle? Would it be difficult? Oddly enough, we lived Cradle to Cradle not too long ago. What can we learn by looking back at these methods—to the time when Cradle to Cradle was just an everyday part of our lives? And there are still cultures that live almost completely in this way. What might we learn by studying them?

Just remember our multitudes of ant friends. They have highly functional systems that have kept their communities green and thriving for ages—right at our feet! The answers to a better tomorrow may be waiting in our own backyards.

> 4. HOW DO YOU PREDICT THE FUTURE?

It's not easy to make predictions about the future out of nothing and nowhere. But if you use your imagination, you can get pretty far. For example, think about something unpleasant that happened to you in the last few days. Maybe you had a flat tire on your bicycle. Do you think this will still happen in twenty years, or will tires be so good that they'll never go flat? Will bikes still have tires? Will there be bikes?

Perhaps you had a bad grade for a test. Is doing your homework and studying boring you? Maybe this will change in the future. You'll learn your lessons with exciting video games or a fun robot teacher that explains everything to you. What do you think?

Maybe you hurt your arm while skateboarding. Who knows, maybe there will be airbags for skateboards in the future that prevent you from hitting the ground. Does that sound crazy? There are already airbag helmets for bicyclists. They are more comfortable than a regular helmet and work better too!

Don't ever worry that your idea sounds crazy. If your idea would improve your life, there is a chance that it will happen one day. And of course, you don't have to create your invention yourself. There's always someone else out there who knows enough about the technology and has the same problem as you. By putting our minds together to pursue a common goal, we have the power to change the world!

> 5. BREAD AND WATER

If you could choose between food that required the killing of an animal or food where no animal was killed or used, what would you choose if they both taste good? What if the food without animal products is healthier and cheaper? And economically and agriculturally better for the world? Do you remember the section on meat alternatives? Do you think we will be eating as much meat or fish in the future as we do today? Will we still eat meat or fish, or not at all? What about bugs; do you think they'll be a common offering on our daily menu?

If smart ovens and microwaves can cook like top chefs in the future, what kind of effects will this have? You could put them on busy streets and in the mall. Anyone who is hungry could choose from hundreds of dishes, put in some money, and then the cooking machine would prepare a fresh and healthy meal within minutes. Do you think it's likely that we'll have these kinds of machines? Or will people always prefer a human cook? Or will people prefer the machine over a cook, who you can only hope washes his hands regularly?

When you see commercials on television, what do you see more of: commercials for candy and junk food or for fruits and vegetables? How many people do you know would like to be skinnier than they are now? Do you think it will be possible to make candy and junk food without all that sugar and fat? How will it affect how people look? And how will it affect their health?

> 6. SICK DAYS IN THE FUTURE? GOODBYE!

In fairy tales and old legends, there is often a so-called "Fountain of Youth." It doesn't exist, of course, but with the exponential progress of science, keeping us young and healthy is becoming more and more of a reality. Imagine if there were a medication that would stop the aging process in our bodies. What would be the consequences for the world?

People no longer have to die of old age. The population will increase enormously. Is that possible? Will there be enough food for everyone? If a pill that keeps everyone young is created, should you be able to take it if it means others will die because of food shortages? Or is it wrong not to have such a pill, causing lots of people to die of old age? If old people stay fit and healthy longer, should they continue to work? Will there be enough work for everyone to do?

Do you think there will be viruses that can cause lots of people to die? Or do you think that doctors will learn how to prevent these kinds of viruses from spreading in the future?

Will it become possible to replace your brain, or part of it, by a machine? If so, will you still be *you*? Would you want to have it if it made you a lot smarter? Or would you never do it because it's a scary thought to have a machine as your brain?

> 7. THE AGE OF THE ROBOT

Machines will always be better in the future than they are in the present. So if you want to come up with the car of the future, you have to look at what's wrong with cars right now. Cars are bad for the environment, but they'll most likely be better in 2030. Lots of accidents happen with cars, but this will improve by 2030 too. Long car trips are boring and uncomfortable, even though the addition of on-board DVD players has alleviated this for passengers. What will car-trip monotony be like in 2030—the same? What else can be improved about today's cars? Think of as many improvements as possible, and imagine what the cars of the future will be like.

Now, let's consider humanoid robots. Do you believe that there will be large-scale production of them by 2030? What could you use them for? Do you think we'll all have robots in our homes? What chores could they do?

You can already buy drones in some stores: little navigational helicopters with a camera. These drones will be so cheap in a few years that most people will be able to afford them. Is your roof leaking? A drone can show you what's wrong. Do you want some nice pictures of your holiday destination? A drone can take pictures from the air. What else can you think of for these flying machines?

One of those invisibility suits . . . That would be good for people in the army or perhaps for police officers. But who else? Would criminals want them too? And terrorists? It sounds neat, but should such a suit really be made? Won't bad people use them more than good people? Should we stop the research and development of invisibility suits? What happens if other people create it first?

Finally: if one more invention needed to be made—one invention to end a problem that you often have—what invention would that be? Imagine the best and most amazing invention for you in the future. Maybe someone will make it for you . . . .

NOTES

Note: unless otherwise noted, web sources were accessed in September of 2013.

Why Should You Be Reading This Book?

1. Peter Patau, "According to Yogi Berra, or Niels Bohr, or Albert Einstein, or Mark Twain, or Somebody," *Letter from Here* (blog), December 2, 2006, http://www.peterpatau.com/2006/12/bohr-leads-berra-but-yogi-closing-gap.html.

Technology Everywhere

1. If you want to learn more about the Y2K arachnophobia that struck worldwide in 1999, *Encyclopedia Britannica Online* has some good background info: http://www.britannica.com/EBchecked/topic/382740/Y2K-bug.

2. The width of the United States, from the East Coast to the West, is 2,680 miles: http://www.worldatlas.com/webimage/countrys/namerica/usstates/uslandst.htm.

3. Measuring at the equator, the Earth's circumference is 24,901.55 miles: http://geography.about.com/od/learnabouttheearth/a/earthfacts.htm.

4. The distance from the Earth to the sun is 92.96 million miles, which means a round-trip would be twice that amount (185.92 million miles): http://www.universetoday.com/66509/how-many-miles-is-the-earth-from-the-sun/. At 33 days, your one-way trip to school is a whopping 1,073,741,824 miles, so you actually have miles to spare if you were to use those same miles on a sixth trip to the sun—but not enough to make it back to Earth again.

5. "History of Computers," University of Rhode Island website: http://homepage.cs.uri.edu/faculty/wolfe/book/Readings/Reading03.htm; "A Brief History of the Computer," Seattle Central Community College website: http://www.seattlecentral.edu/~ymoh/history_of_computer/history_of_computer.htm.

6. Jonathan Strickland, "How Moore's Law Works," HowStuffWorks.com: http://computer.howstuffworks.com/moores-law.htm.

7. "Cost of Hard Drive Storage Space," Nova Scotia's Electric Gleaner: http://ns1758.ca/winch/winchest.html; Matt Komorowski, "A History of Storage Cost," mkomo.com: http://www.mkomo.com/cost-per-gigabyte.

And in case you're wondering about how data storage units (or bytes) are broken down, it looks like this:

1 kilobyte (kB) = 1000 bytes

1 megabyte (MB) = 1,000,000 bytes (or 1000 kilobytes)

1 gigabyte (GB) = 1,000,000,000 bytes (or 1000 megabytes)

(Source: "What Units of Measurement Are Used for Data Storage?" TechTerms.com Help Center: http://www.techterms .com/help/data_storage_units_of_measurement).

8. See note 6 on the left.

Chapter 1

1. The idea of maximizing land, food supply, and water use by incorporating agriculture into a variety of built environments is called "building-integrated agriculture," or BIA. There are a number of online discussions dedicated to this, like the University of Washington's Department of Architecture blog: http://uwarch -belog.com/index.php/2012/12/building-integrated-agriculture/.

2. "A Historic Opportunity," Architecture 2030 website: http:// architecture2030.org/the_solution/buildings_solution_how#.

There's a lot more information about Architecture 2030's mission, work, and other contributions on the organization's website: architecture2030.org.

3. Glen Tickle, "New Technique Hijacks Photosynthesis to Create Electricity from Plants," GeekSystem.com (May 11, 2013): http://www.geekosystem.com/electricity-from-photosynthesis/.

4. Olivia Solon, "Leaf-Shaped Solar Panels Could Coat Building Like Ivy," *Wired* UK website (July 11, 2011): http://www.wired.co.uk/news/archive/2011-07/11/solar-ivy.

5. "Electronic paper" definition, *PC Magazine* online encyclopedia: http://www.pcmag.com/encyclopedia/term/42494/electronic-paper.

6. Bonny Wolf, "Kitchens of the Future Will Really Know How to Cook," NPR online (August 18, 2013): http://www.npr.org/2013/08/18/213055078/kitchens-of-the-future-will-really-know-how-to-cook.

Take a look at this slideshow of eleven future products that are in the works now, like the Bio Robot Refrigerator that cools with a biopolymer gel, and the LG Blast Chiller, which is said to chill your can of soda in five minutes: http://www.pcmag.com/slideshow/story/303627/the-kitchen-of-the-future (Meredith

Popolo, "The Kitchen of the Future," *PC Magazine* website, October 12, 2012).

7. This device is called the Nutri-Pulse, and it uses electric pulses to cook food: http://www.innovation-xl.com/en/nutripulse.html.

8. In chapter 1, note 6 (on the facing page), the first item featured in *PC Magazine*'s online slideshow is called the Gaggenau FreeInduction Cooktop, and it uses forty-eight micro-inductors of oscillating magnetic fields in a large stovetop that can accommodate up to four pans placed anywhere on its surface: http://www.pcmag.com/slideshow/story/303627/the-kitchen-of-the-future/1. The inductors only heat where they're needed, leaving the rest of the surface cool to the touch—a much safer way to cook.

9. "What Is Water Scarcity?" The Water Project website: http://thewaterproject.org/water_scarcity.php; "Water Conservation," EPA website: http://www.epa.gov/oaintrnt/water/; "Water Conservation Tips," *National Geographic* website: http://environment.nationalgeographic.com/environment/freshwater/water-conservation-tips/.

10. Catharine Smith, "High-Tech Toilets: Amazing Bathrooms from the Future" slideshow, HuffingtonPost.com (April 24, 2010): http://www.huffingtonpost.com/2010/02/22/future-bathrooms-amazing_n_471219.html.

Chapter 2

1. Department of Economic and Social Affairs, *World Population to 2300* (New York, NY: United Nations, 2004), 5.

2. At the original Earth Day in 1970, ecologist Kenneth Watt predicted, "By the year 2000, if present trends continue, we will be using up crude oil at such a rate . . . that there won't be any more crude oil." (Ronald Bailey, "Earth Day, Then and Now," Reason Online [May 1, 2000]: http://reason.com/archives/2000/05/01/earth-day-then-and-now/print).

3. According to the same article in the above note (note 2), "The US Geological Survey estimates . . . that global reserves could be as much as 2.1 trillion barrels of crude oil—enough to supply the world for the next ninety years."

4. "Issues—Oil," David Suzuki Foundation website: http://www.davidsuzuki.org/issues/climate-change/science/energy/oil/.

5. Coal is available in about seventy countries worldwide, with some of the largest reserves in the United States. The World Coal Association estimates, however, that there is actually only 112 years of coal available at current production rates. ("Where Is Coal Found?" World Coal Association website: http://www.worldcoal.org/coal/where-is-coal-found/). This readily available supply reduces energy costs but at what environmental cost?

6. The Global Education Project has this to say about coal versus oil: "The energy stored in oil is significantly greater than in any other currently available source. There is no other equivalently cheap and powerful energy...." ("World Energy Supply," The Global Education Project: http://www.theglobaleducationproject. org/earth/energy-supply.php).

7. As of September 2013, the World Nuclear Association reports that there is enough uranium available worldwide to meet predicted demands for a few more decades—but not for half a century. ("Uranium Supply and Demand in Balance for Now," World Nuclear News [September 12, 2013]: http://www .world-nuclear-news.org/ENF-Uranium_supply_and_demand_ in_balance_for_now-1209137s.html).

8. M. Lagi, Yavni Bar-Yam, K. Z. Bertrand, and Yaneer Bar-Yam, "The Food Crises: A Quantitative Model of Food Prices, Including Speculators and Ethanol Conversion," New England Complex Systems Institute (September 21, 2011): http://necsi.edu/research/ social/foodprices.html.

9. Marc Lallanilla, "How Do Wind Turbines Kill Birds?" LiveScience.com (May 14, 2013): http://www.livescience.com/ 31995-how-do-wind-turbines-kill-birds.html.

10. Allen Chen, "New Study Finds that the Price of Wind Energy in the United States Is Near an All-Time Low," Berkeley Lab

Online News Center (August 6, 2013): http://newscenter.lbl.gov/
news-releases/2013/08/06/new-study-finds-that-the-price-of-wind
-energy-in-the-united-states-is-near-an-all-time-low/.

11. "How Much Solar Energy Hits Earth?" EcoWorld.com (June
14, 2006): http://www.ecoworld.com/energy-fuels/how-much-
solar-energy-hits-earth.html.

12. According to SolarPanelCostGuide.com, the average home's
electric use is 20–24 kWh per day. The solar panels necessary to
meet this demand would cost $15K–$20K after installation, which
pays for itself in about ten years (at an average of five hours of
sunlight a day and at a 5 percent financing discount): http://
www.solarpanelscostguide.com/#cost.

13. "Why It's the End of the Line for Wind Power," Forbes.com
(December 21, 2012): http://www.forbes.com/sites/
christopherhelman/2012/12/21/why-its-the-end-of-the-line-for
-wind-power/.

14. "Getting Wind Farms Off the Ground," *The Economist*
Technology Quarterly (June 6, 2007): http://www.economist
.com/node/9249242; Lisa Zyga, "Kites Could Provide
Electricity for 100,000 Homes," Phys.org (August 8, 2008):
http://phys.org/news137388314.html.

15. Check out this video of Saul Griffith's 2009 TED Talk, in which he explains more about high-altitude wind energy from kites: http://www.ted.com/talks/saul_griffith_on_kites_as_the_future_of_renewable_energy.html.

16. Current energy usage worldwide is 18,443 TWh (terawatt hours, or 1000-watt hours), and it is projected to increase to 35,000 TWh by 2035. With 11 percent coming from nuclear energy (or 2,028 TWh), we will need roughly seventeen times more nuclear power. ("World Energy Needs and Nuclear Power," World Nuclear Association website: http://www.world-nuclear. org/info/Current-and-Future-Generation/World-Energy-Needs-and-Nuclear-Power/#.UjY5_4VcQ7D).

17. "Nuclear Fusion Power," World Nuclear Association website: http://www.world-nuclear.org/info/Current-and-Future-Generation/Nuclear-Fusion-Power/#.UjY_w4VcQ7A.

18. "Future Energy Technology," Alternative Energy News website: http://www.alternative-energy-news.info/technology/future-energy/.

19. "Volkswagen Beetle," Wikipedia.org: http://en.wikipedia.org/wiki/Volkswagen_Beetle; Holly Richmond, "Record-Breaking Volkswagen Is More Fuel Efficient Than Your Hybrid," Grist.org

(June 26, 2013): http://grist.org/list/volkswagen-passat-tdi
-breaks-mileage-record/.

20. "Université Laval Regains Fuel-Efficiency Title," Shell.com
(April 8, 2013): http://www.shell.com/global/environment
-society/ecomarathon/events/americas/media/2012/
universite-laval-regains-fuel-efficiency-title.html.

21. Joel Kirkland and Climatewire, "Global Emissions Predicted
to Grow through 2035," ScientificAmerican.com (May 26, 2010):
http://www.scientificamerican.com/article.cfm?id=global
-emissions-predicted-to-grow.

22. "Global Temperature Rise Could Reach 10 Degrees
Fahrenheit by 2100, Report Finds," HuffingtonPost.com
(November 8, 2012): http://www.huffingtonpost.com
/2012/11/08/global-temperature-rise_n_2094996.html.

23. Douglas Fischer, "Even Deep Cuts in Greenhouse Gas
Emissions Will Not Stop Global Warming," ScientificAmerican
.com (April 14, 2009): http://www.scientificamerican.com/
article.cfm?id=even-deep-cuts-in-greenho.

24. K. R. Briffa, P. D. Jones, F. H. Schweingruber, and
T. J. Osborn, "Influence of Volcanic Eruptions on Northern

Hemisphere Temperatures Over the Past 600 Years," Letters to
Nature, *Nature* 393 (June 4, 1998), 450–455 (http://www
.nature.com/nature/journal/v393/n6684/abs/393450a0.html);
Wynne Parry, "20 Years After Pinatubo: How Volcanoes Could
Alter Climate," LiveScience.com (June 9, 2011): http://www
.livescience.com/14513-pinatubo-volcano-future-climate
-change-eruption.html.

25. Erik Klemetti, "Artificial Volcanoes Are Not the Solution
to Warming," Wired.com (July 19, 2012): http://www.wired.com
/wiredscience/2012/07/artificial-volcanoes-arent-the-solution-to
-warming/; "Sulphate Aerosols & Artificial Volcanoes," Hands Off
Mother Earth website: http://www.handsoffmotherearth.org/
about/.

Chapter 3

1. To date, we've lost 27 percent of the world's coral reefs
forever, and 30 percent more are at risk if current destruction
rates are not addressed within the next thirty years. That's
actually *more* than half of the world's coral reefs, which directly
impacts global fisheries, tourism, marine wildlife diversity, and
shoreline protection. Did you know that reefs are where 25
percent of *all* known ocean fish species live? Coral reefs are
pretty important—to all of us! ("Fast Facts: Why Coral Reefs

Are Important to People," WWF [World Wildlife Fund] Global website: http://wwf.panda.org/about_our_earth/blue_planet/coasts/coral_reefs/coral_facts/).

2. "Our Work: Responsible Forestry Overview," WWF (World Wildlife Fund) website: http://worldwildlife.org/industries/responsible-forestry; "Threats: Deforestation Overview," WWF (World Wildlife Fund) website: http://worldwildlife.org/threats/deforestation.

3. According to the World Wildlife Fund, global deforestation contributes to about 15 percent of all greenhouse gas emissions. ("Habitats: Forests Overview," WWF website: http://worldwildlife.org/habitats/forests.)

4. Gregory Berns, "The Stupidity of Crowds," *plus2sd* (blog), *Psychology Today* website, September 23, 2008, http://www.psychologytoday.com/blog/plus2sd/200809/the-stupidity-crowds; Johan Lehrer, "When We're Cowed by the Crowd," *The Wall Street Journal* website (May 28, 2011): http://online.wsj.com/article/SB10001424052702304066504576341280447107102.html?mod=djkeyword; "Groupthink," Wikipedia.org: http://en.wikipedia.org/wiki/Groupthink.

5. Carl Zimmer, "Bringing Them Back to Life," *National Geographic* website (April 2013): http://ngm.nationalgeographic.com/2013/04/125-species-revival/zimmer-text.

6. Dan Nosowitz, "Japanese Researchers Announce Plan to Resurrect Woolly Mammoth Within Five Years," *Popular Science* website (January 18, 2011): http://www.popsci.com/science/ article/2011-01/japanese-researchers-plan-resurrect-woolly -mammoth-within-five-years.

7. "C2C Framework," McDonough Braungart Design Chemistry website: http://www.mbdc.com/cradle-to-cradle/c2c-framework/; *Cradle to Cradle* book review, Make Wealth History website (January 17, 2011): http://makewealthhistory.org/2011/01/17/ cradle-to-cradle-by-michael-braungart-and-william-mcdonough/.

8. Ina Röpcke, "The Solar House Concept is Spreading," *Sun & Wind Energy* (September 2011): 42–47 (http://www.jenni .ch/pdf/SunWindEnergy.pdf; graphic of thermal energy aquifer: http://4.bp.blogspot.com/-QsPBMX3zxnc/TePbgcBFTSI/ AAAAAAAAm4/rN3gkXiJ_70/s400/Aquifer%2BThermal %2BEnergy%2BStorage.jpg).

9. The size of Spain and Portugal combined has been compared to the size of the Great Pacific Garbage Patch, which is three times as big. And since Spain is about 1.19 times the size of California, the patch is also as large as about three Californias ("The Great Pacific Garbage Patch," 5W Infographics [2010]: http://visual.ly/great-pacific-garbage-patch; MapFight online app: http://mapfight.appspot.com/california-vs-es/ california-us-spain-size-comparison).

10. Plastics account for 90 percent of ocean waste, and whether in whole or broken-down forms, they are impossible for marine fish and wildlife to digest. Greenpeace estimates that 1 million birds and 100,000 marine mammals die each year due to plastic ingestion, with 267 species affected. (Maxime Goualin, "Ocean Garbage Patches: Plastic Waste and Marine Debris Threaten the Future of Marine Life," Cereplast.com [March 16, 2011]: http://www.cereplast.com/ocean-garbage -patches-plastic-waste-and-marine-debris-threaten-the-future -of-marine-life/) This includes sharks and whales, and mass extinction looms if pollution practices are left to fester. (Fiona Harvey, "'Shocking' State of Seas Threatens Mass Extinction, Say Marine Experts," *The Guardian* website [June 20, 2011]: http://www.theguardian.com/environment/2011/jun/20/ marine-life-oceans-extinction-threat).

11. Kirsten Hendrich, "Rare Earth Elements Infographic Shows the Impact of Resource Depletion on Green Technology," Inhabitat.com (December 3, 2012): http://inhabitat.com/ rare-earth-elements-infographic-shows-the-impact-of-resource -depletion-on-green-technology/; "China Warns Its Rare Earth Reserves Are Declining," BBC.com (June 20, 2012): http://www.bbc.co.uk/news/business-18516461.

Chapter 4

1. "About James Randi," James Randi Educational Foundation

website: http://www.randi.org/site/index.php/about-james
-randi.html.

2. Robert Strohmeyer, "The 7 Worst Tech Predictions of All Time,"
TechHive.com (December 31, 2008): http://www.techhive.com/
article/155984/worst_tech_predictions.html.

3. Andrew Hamilton, "Brains That Click," *Popular Mechanics*
March 1949): 258 (http://books.google.com/books?id=w9gDAA
AAMBAJ&lpg=PA162&dq=popular%20mechanics%201949%20
computers&pg=PA258%23v=onepage& q&f=false#v=onepage
&q=popular%20mechanics%201949%20computers&f=false).

4. "Hitler & WWII (Quatrain 2-24)," The Nostradamus Society of
America website: http://www.nostradamususa.com/hitler.html.

5. Gordon Goble, "Top 10 Bad Tech Predictions," DigitalTrends
.com (November 4, 2012): http://www.digitaltrends.com/
features/top-10-bad-tech-predictions/4/.

6. Mitchell Stephens, "History of Television," *Grolier Multimedia
Encyclopedia*, 2000 ed.: http://www.nyu.edu/classes/stephens/
History%20of%20Television%20page.htm.

7. Vivek Wadhwa, "Is iPhone 5S Version 1 of the Star Trek
Tricorder?" WRAL TechWire.com (September 16, 2013): http://
wraltechwire.com/vivek-for-monday/12883244/.

8. Florian Mueller, "Samsung Cites Stanley Kubrick's *2001: A Space Odyssey* Movie as Prior Art Against iPad Design Patent," *Foss Patents* (blog), August 23, 2011, http://www.fosspatents .com/2011/08/samsung-cites-stanley-kubricks-2001.html.

9. An estimated 20 to 40 million people died worldwide as a result of the 1918 Spanish flu pandemic—one of the worst disasters on record. It became such an everyday part of life that children were reported to skip rope to this related rhyme: "I had a little bird / It's name was Enza. / I opened the window / And in-flu-Enza." (Molly Billings, "The Influenza Pandemic of 1918," Stanford University website [June 1997]: http://virus.stanford. edu/uda/).

10. "A Brief Career Summary of Ray Kurzweil," Kurzweil Technologies website: http://www.kurzweiltech.com/aboutray. html; "Books by Ray Kurzweil: *The Age of Intelligent Machines*," Kurzweil Accelerating Intelligence website (September 8, 2009): http://www.kurzweilai.net/the-age-of-intelligent-machines.

11. Ibid.

12. There is a brief video at *Playmaker Magazine* online of Kurzweil explaining his thoughts on Moore's law and computer technology, which he believes will play out as *exponential* advances in noncomputer technologies (Bradford Harrison, "SXSW 2013 Interactive: Ray Kurzweil," *Playmaker Magazine*

online [March 13, 2012]: http://www.playmakeronline
.com/2012/03/13/sxsw-2012-interactive-ray-kurzweil/.

13. Ray Kurzweil was a speaker at the 2013 Global Future 2045
International Congress in New York. This three-minute video sheds
light on where his "immortality by 2045" predictions originate:
http://www.kurzweilai.net/global-futures-2045-ray-kurzweil
-immortality-by-2045 (Kurzweil Accelerating Intelligence website
[June 21, 2013]). This is the second year for the congress, which is
hosted by the Global Future 2045 Initiative, a movement founded
by Russian entrepreneur Dmitry Itskov in 2011. Its goal: "to create
technologies enabling the transfer of a individual's personality
to a more advanced nonbiological carrier and extending life,
including to the point of immortality. We devote particular attention
to enabling the fullest possible dialogue between the world's
major spiritual traditions, science, and society." ("About Us" page,
GF2045.com: http://www.gf2045.com/about/).

14. Pure Home Water (PHW) website and video: http://
purehomewater.org/.

15. "7 Radical Energy Solutions, Made Interactive," *Scientific
American* website (May 16, 2011): http://www.scientificamerican
.com/article.cfm?id=radical-energy-solutions-interactive.

16. "Bayes' theorem," Wikipedia.org: http://en.wikipedia.org/
wiki/Bayes%27_theorem.

Chapter 5

1. Cocoa (Cote d'Ivoire): "Major Exporting Countries of Cocoa Products [in 2011]," APEDA Agri Exchange website: http://agriexchange.apeda.gov.in/product_profile/Major_Exporing_Countries.aspx?categorycode=0504; coffee (Brazil): "Top 10 Coffee Exporting Countries by Production [in 2011]," MapsofWorld.com: http://www.mapsofworld.com/world-maps/top-coffee-exporting-countries.html; soybeans (Paraguay): "Soybeans—World Supply and Demand Summary," Spectrum Commodities website: http://www.spectrumcommodities.com/education/commodity/statistics/soybeans.html; corn (Argentina): "Corn—World Supply and Demand Summary," Spectrum Commodities website: http://www.spectrumcommodities.com/education/commodity/statistics/corn.html; cotton (Uzbekistan): "Cotton—World Supply and Demand Summary," Spectrum Commodities website: http://www.spectrumcommodities.com/education/commodity/statistics/cotton.html.

A recent example of the negative influence of rich countries on the culture and livelihood of poor export countries is that of Bolivia and the popular grain quinoa. Though its demand has increased the payout to farmers, local residents can no longer afford the cost of the native grain, resorting to cheaper, processed foods and increasing malnutrition rates as a result. (Simon Romero, "Quinoa's Global Success Creates Quandry at Home," *New York Times* website [March 19, 2011]: http://www.nytimes.com/2011/03/20/world/ americas/20bolivia.html?_r=0).

2. "Water for Agriculture and Nutrition," *World Savvy Monitor* (November 2009): http://worldsavvy.org/monitor/index .php?option=com_content&view=article&id=711&Itemid=1197; Eric Holt-Giménez, "The World Food Crisis: What Is Behind It and What We Can Do," *Hunger Notes* online publication, World Hunger Education Service (WHES) (October 23, 2008): http:// www.worldhunger.org/articles/09/editorials/holt-gimenez.htm.

3. To learn about how much water it takes to raise all sorts of products, from coffee to cotton to sheep, flip through this informative gallery at WaterFootprint.org: http://www .waterfootprint.org/?page=files/productgallery.

4. Tom Philpott, "Want to Avoid a Thirsty Future? Eat Less Meat," *Mother Jones* website (August 29, 2012): http://www.motherjones.com/tom-philpott/2012/08/ want-avoid-thirsty-future-eat-less-meat.

If you want a clearer idea of just how much meat Americans eat, check out the American Meat Institute website: "The United States Meat Industry at a Glance," http://www.meatami.com/ht/d/ sp/i/47465/pid/47465.

5. "The Consequences of Eating Meat," AnimalFreedom.org: http://www.animalfreedom.org/english/information/ meat.html.

6. "Meat Production Wastes Natural Resources," PETA website: http://www.peta.org/issues/animals-used-for-food/meat-wastes -natural-resources.aspx.

7. Elisabeth Rosenthal, "Rush to Use Crops as Fuel Raises Food Prices and Hunger Fears," *New York Times* website (April 6, 2011): http://www.nytimes.com/2011/04/07/science/ earth/07cassava.html.

Something like the potential biofuel/food crisis already happened with the rice crisis in 2008: http://www.npr.org/blogs/thesalt/ 2011/11/02/141771712/how-fear-drove-world-rice-markets -insane (Dan Charles, "How Fear Drove World Rice Markets Insane," *The Salt* (blog), NPR.org, November 2, 2011).

8. Stephanie Strom, "China's Food Deal Extends Its Reach, Already Mighty," *New York Times* website (May 29, 2013): http://www.nytimes.com/2013/05/30/business/wariness-over -a-deal-intended-to-deliver-more-pork-to-china.html?pagewanted =all&_r=0; Mark Fischetti, "US Demand for Fruits and Vegetables Drives Up Imports," *Scientific American* online (September 12, 2013): http://www.scientificamerican.com/article.cfm?id=us -demand-for-fruits-and-vegetables-drives-up-imports.

9. "How Far Does Your Food Travel to Get to Your Plate?" CUESA (Center for Urban Education about Sustainable Agriculture) website: http://www.cuesa.org/page/ how-far-does-your-food-travel-get-your-plate.

10. Celia W. Dugger, "Half the World Soon to Be in Cities," *New York Times* website (June 27, 2007): http://www.nytimes .com/2007/06/27/world/27cnd-population.html.

11. John Vidal, "UN Warns of Looming Worldwide Food Crisis in 2013," *The Observer*, *The Guardian* website (October 13, 2012): http://www.theguardian.com/global-development/2012/oct/14/ un-global-food-crisis-warning.

12. "Tour the Hi-Tech Farm That's Growing 100 Tons of Greens On the Roof of a Brooklyn Warehouse," BrightFarms blog, BrightFarms.com (July 27, 2011): http://blog.brightfarms.com/ TourTheHiTechFarmThatsGrowing100TonsOfGreensOnThe RoofOfABrooklynWarehouse.

13. "VertiCrop™ Is a Revolutionary Growing System Selected in 2009 by *Time* Magazine as One of the World's Greatest Inventions," Alterrus website: http://www.alterrus.ca/verticrop/ the-technology/.

Alterrus Systems, Inc., the innovative Vancouver company that created VertiCrop™, is a certified "B corporation." The

B-corporation collective is new, global, and growing in its mission to "use the power of business to solve social and environmental problems" (bcorporation.net).

14. Glenn Zorpette, "A Consumer's Guide to Fake Meat," *IEEE Spectrum* website (June 3, 2013): http://spectrum.ieee.org/geek-life/hands-on/a-consumers-guide-to-fake-meat.

15. "How Do Different Color Filters Affect Plant Growth?" UCSB ScienceLine website: http://scienceline.ucsb.edu/getkey.php?key=3155; "7. How Much Energy Can Be Saved Using Supplemental LED Lighting?" FAQ page, *LED Lighting for Specialty-Crop Production* research project website: http://leds.hrt.msu.edu/FAQs/.

16. The "Frankenstein" metaphor is popular in the United Kingdom, where they fiercely oppose GM food. (Fiona Macrae, "Frankenstein Food Firm 'Quits' Europe: US Giant Surrenders in Face of Public Suspicion Over Its Pesticide-Resistant GM Crops," *Daily Mail* online [July 18, 2013]: http://www.dailymail.co.uk/news/article-2369722/Frankenstein-food-firm-quits-Europe-U-S-giant-surrenders-face-public-suspicion-pesticide-resistant-GM-crops.html).

17. "Blue Strawberries, Genetically Modified by Fish Genes—Fact Analysis," Hoax or Fact website (July 5, 2013): http://www

.hoaxorfact.com/Science/blue-strawberries-genetically-modified
-by-fish-genes-facts-analysis.html.

18. "Should We Grow GM Crops?" *Harvest of Fear*, Nova/
Frontline Special Report website (2001): http://www.pbs.org/
wgbh/harvest/exist/arguments.html.

19. "*Atlantic Dawn*: The Ship from Hell," British Sea Fishing
website: http://britishseafishing.co.uk/atlantic-dawn-the-ship
-from-hell/.

The *Atlantic Dawn* is currently owned by a Dutch consortium
that renamed it the *Annelies Ilena*, and you can track its current
position via MarineTraffic.com: http://www.marinetraffic.com/
ais/shipdetails.aspx?mmsi=244563000.

20. "The Five Threats—Threat 1: Overfishing," Save
Our Seas Foundation website: http://saveourseas.com/
threats/overfishing#1; Longlining info page, Sea Shepherd
Conservation Society website: http://www.seashepherd.org/
sharks/longlining.html.

Another big issue is all the fishing gear—or "ghost gear"—
abandoned in the ocean by the fishing industry. Estimates are
that 10 to 15 percent of each boat's gear is lost annually, which
causes both unseen and recurring damage to marine wildlife,

including birds. (Kurt Lieber, "The Deadliest Ghosts," Mission Blue website [February 20, 2013]: http://mission-blue.org/2013/02/the-deadliest-ghosts/).

21. See note 20 above, "The Five Threats." And if you have the time, there is a powerful, hour-long documentary called *Sea the Truth*, which was produced by the Nicolaas G. Pierson Foundation: http://www.seathetruth.nl/en/.

22. "Global Challenges Facing Humanity—2. Water: How Can Everybody Have Sufficient Clean Water Without Conflict?" The Millennium Project website (2012): http://www.millennium-project.org/millennium/Global_Challenges/chall-02.html.

23. Ibid.

24. See the handy WaterFootprint.org product gallery first mentioned in note 3 (in this chapter) for a refresher on the *water* costs of growing things—of agriculture.

Manufacturing your laptop (which includes the mining of rare metals for its components) requires up to 2,800 gallons of water, or the equivalent of washing about seventy loads of laundry! (See chapter 3, note 11, "China Warns Its Rare Earth Reserves Are Declining"; Dennis Nelson, "Six Ways We All Use Water Without Knowing It," Mother Nature Network website: http://www.mnn.com/food/beverages/sponsorstory/

six-ways-we-all-use-water-without-knowing-it; "Consumer Energy
Center: Clothes Washers," California Energy Commission
website: http://www.consumerenergycenter.org/home/
appliances/washers.html).

The competition for water is already being felt in the United
States (let alone other, poorer parts of the world), which is
raising concerns about future water supplies globally. (Patrik
Jonsson, "Drought: Farmers Dig Deeper, Water Tables Drop,
Competition Heats Up," *The Christian Science Monitor*
website [August 8, 2012]: http://www.csmonitor.com/
USA/2012/0808/Drought-Farmers-dig-deeper-water-tables
-drop-competition-heats-up).

25. Susan L. Nasr, "How the Slingshot Water Purifier Works,"
HowStuffWorks.com: http://science.howstuffworks.com/
environmental/green-tech/remediation/slingshot-water-purifier.htm;
"Our Founder [Dean Kamen]," DEKA Research and Development
website: http://www.dekaresearch.com/founder.shtml.

26. The idea of corn shrimp, crickos, and bugburgers comes
from a cool children's book called *Man Eating Bugs: The Art
and Science of Eating Insects,* by Peter Menzel and Faith
D'Aluisio (Ten Speed Press [Berkeley, CA: 2004]: http://
www.amazon.com/Man-Eating-Bugs-Science-Insects/dp/
1580080227/ref=sr_1_1?s=books&ie=UTF8&qid=1380557834&
sr=1-1&keywords=man+eating+bugs%2C+ten+speed+press).

27. Damian Carrington, "Insects Could Be the Key to Meeting Food Needs of Growing Global Population," *The Observer, The Guardian* website (July 31, 2010): http://www.theguardian.com/environment/2010/aug/01/insects-food-emissions.

28. "Kitchen," Wikipedia.org: http://en.wikipedia.org/wiki/Kitchen; Gina Salamone, "Get Cooking Guys: Men Have More Than Doubled Time in the Kitchen Preparing Meals Since 1961," *New York Daily News* website (August 18, 2009): http://www.nydailynews.com/life-style/eats/cooking-guys-men-doubled-time-kitchen-preparing-meals-1961-article-1.396872.

29. Superfood expert and health guru David Wolfe came out with a book in 2009—*Superfoods: The Food and Medicine of the Future*—that emphasizes "the pivotal role of superfoods in promoting nutritional excellence; health and well-being; beauty enhancement; sustainable agriculture; and the transformation of diet, lifestyle, and planet." (http://www.amazon.com/Superfoods-Medicine-Future-David-Wolfe/dp/1556437765/ref=sr_1_3?ie=UTF8&s=books&qid=1243122122&sr=8-3)

30. Obesity data and statistics page, CDC.gov (updated January 11, 2013): http://www.cdc.gov/obesity/data/childhood.html; Sharon Begley, "Fat and Getting Fatter: US Obesity Rates to Soar by 2030," Reuters.com (September 8, 2012): http://www.reuters.com/article/2012/09/18/us-obesity-us-idUSBRE88H0RA20120918.

31. Michaeleen Doucleff, "The Cotton Candy Grape: A Sweet Spin on Designer Fruit," *The Salt* (blog), NPR.org, August 6, 2013, http://www.npr.org/blogs/thesalt/2013/08/05/209222126/the-cotton-candy-grape-a-sweet-spin-on-designer-fruit.

32. Mo Rocca, "The Future of Candy," *The Tomorrow Show*, CBSnews.com (September 13, 2009): http://www.cbsnews.com/video/watch/?id=5306845n.

33. Alexandra Sifferlin, "New Genes [Identified] in Obesity: How Much of Weight is Genetic?" *Time Healthland* (blog), Time.com, July 19, 2013, http://healthland.time.com/2013/07/19/news-genes-idd-in-obesity-how-much-of-weight-is-genetic/.

Chapter 6

1. Daniel Kraft, "Exponential Technologies Across Health Care," Kauffman Fellows Report 2 (2011): http://kauffmanfellows.org/journal_posts/exponential-technologies-across-health-care/.

2. To date, there have been a number of stem-cell advances and victories, including one involving a woman with a rare form of leukemia who has outlived the survival rate by more than three years, and another that involves a new stem-cell-generated windpipe for a little girl. (Kristen Zambo, "A Stem Cell Success Story," *The Journal Times* website [July 18, 2012]: http://

journaltimes.com/lifestyles/health-med-fit/a-stem-cell-success-story/article_cfef3c64-d032-11e1-96e1-001a4bcf887a.html); Lindsey Tanner, "Two-Year-Old Girl Gets Windpipe Made from Stem Cells," *USA Today* online (April 30, 2013): http://www.usatoday.com/story/news/nation/2013/04/30/girl-windpipe-stem-cells/2123881/.

3. Richard A. D'Aveni, "3-D Printing Will Change the World," *Harvard Business Review* online (March 2013): http://hbr.org/2013/03/3-d-printing-will-change-the-world/.

4. "Making a Bit of Me: A Machine that Prints Organs Is Coming to Market," *The Economist* online (February 18, 2010): http://www.economist.com/node/15543683.

Check out this video on Time.com about how "An Inkjet Saved My Bladder!": http://content.time.com/time/video/player/0,32068,1276240844_1681557,00.html.

5. "About the Flu: H1N1," Flu.gov: http://www.flu.gov/about_the_flu/h1n1/#; see also chapter 4, note 9.

6. "Table 22. Life Expectancy at Birth, at 65 Years of Age, at 75 Years of Age, by Race and Sex: United States, Selected Years 1900–2007," Trend Tables, *Health, United States, 2010 Report*, CDC.gov: www.cdc.gov/nchs/data/hus/2010/022.pdf. (Note that race can affect these expectancies, both in the past and currently.)

7. (This first resource includes a video.) Dhiya Kuriakose, "New Technology Allows the Mind to Control Prosthetic Limbs," Mashable.com (June 14, 2013): http://mashable.com/ 2013/06/14/prosthetic-mind-control/; Isaac Perry Clements, "How Prosthetic Limbs Work," HowStuffWorks.com: http:// science.howstuffworks.com/prosthetic-limb5.htm.

8. Nick McDermott, "Meet Rex, The Real Bionic Man (And He Didn't Cost $6 Million!): Scientists Create Body Using Artificial Limbs and Organs," *Daily Mail* online (January 28, 2013): http:// www.dailymail.co.uk/sciencetech/article-2269824/Scientists -create-bionic-body-using-artificial-limbs-organs.html.

9. Peter Williams, "Exoskeleton Provides Superhuman Strength," TechLife.net (July 22, 2013): http://www.techlife.net/lifestyle/ news/2013/7/wearable-robots-powered-exoskeleton-provides -superhuman-strength/.

Want to see five *real* Iron Man suits? There's a video with this article: "I Am Iron Man: Top 5 Exoskeleton Robots," by David Goldstein (Discovery.com [November 27, 2012]: http://news .discovery.com/tech/robotics/exoskeleton-robots-top-5.htm).

10. Though they are mostly recreational and require a lot of muscle strength, running stilts by Poweriser can get you bolting or jumping at a rate of 18.6 miles per hour (see note 9 above, "Exoskeleton Provides Superhuman Strength"). When combined with other advances like the Honda Walking Assist and Ekso Bionics products, one can only imagine the improvements over time. (Mike Hanlon, "Honda Begins Leasing Walking Assist Exoskeleton," GizMag.com [May 27, 2013]: http://www.gizmag.com/honda-leasing-walking -assist-device-exoskeleton/27681/; Matthew Gannon, "Exoskeleton Allows Paraplegics to Walk," CNN.com [March 22, 2013]: http:// www.cnn.com/2013/03/13/tech/innovation/original-ideas -exoskeleton/index.html).

11. Ewen Callaway, "Dramatic Rejuvenation of Prematurely Aged Mice Hints at Potential Therapy," *Nature* online (November 28, 2010): http://www.nature.com/news/2010/101128/full/ news.2010.635.html.

Chapter 7

1. Cristen Conger, "10 NASA Inventions You Might Use Every Day," *Curiosity* (TV show), Discovery.com: http://dsc.discovery .com/tv-shows/curiosity/topics/ten-nasa-inventions.htm.

The Space Foundation's website offers an extensive list of additional innovations, from 1988 to 2013, in the Space Technology Hall of Fame: http://www.spacefoundation.org/ programs/space-technology-hall-fame/inducted-technologies.

2. Joel Hruska, "Virgin Galactic Successfully Tests Re-entry, Prepares for Space Tourism in 2014," ExtremeTech.com

(September 7, 2013): http://www.extremetech.com/extreme/
165943-virgin-galactic-successfully-tests-re-entry-prepares-for
-space-tourism-in-2014.

3. Dan Leone, "$16.6 Billion NASA Budget Clears House
Panel," Space.com (July 10, 2013): http://www.space
.com/21922-nasa-budget-approved-house-panel.html;
Zaina Adamu, "Exploring Space: Why's It So Important?"
Lightyears (blog), CNN.com, October 20, 2012, http://
lightyears.blogs.cnn.com/ 2012/10/20/exploring-space
-whys-it-so-important/.

4. Adrian Padeanu, "Terrafugia Proves the Transition Is a
'Roadable Aircraft,'" WorldCarFans.com (August 5, 2013):
http://www.worldcarfans.com/113080561088/
terrafugia-proves-the-transition-is-a-roadable-aircraft.

Terrafugia, the company behind the Transition drivable plane,
"intends to catalyze a revolution in personal mobility" by taking
the first steps toward the creation of practical flying cars. The
Transition is its closest model, with a public release slated
for 2015 (at $270,000 each). Their other model, the TF-X, is
expected to take eight to twelve more years before it is ready
and is a "true" flying car, with simple, carlike steering; seating
for four; manual and automatic modes; as well as the ability to
drive regular roads and highways as easily as a regular car.
(Terrafugia.com)

5. Christopher Lampton, "Electric Cars vs. Hydrogen Fuel Cell Cars," HowStuffWorks.com: http://auto.howstuffworks.com/ electric-cars-vs-hydrogen-fuel-cell-cars.htm.

6. Ibid. See also "Hydrogen Basics—Introduction," Florida Solar Energy Center (FSEC) website: http://www.fsec.ucf.edu/en/ consumer/hydrogen/basics/introduction.htm.

7. Wayne Cunningham, "Tesla Battery Swap a Dead End," CNET.com (June 21, 2013): http://reviews.cnet.com/8301 -13746_7-57590471-48/tesla-battery-swap-a-dead-end/.

8. "How Will Smart Cars Affect the Future of Driving?" ScienceDaily.com (October 5, 2012): http://www.sciencedaily .com/releases/2012/10/121005123821.htm.

9. Ben Schiller, "A Road Built Out of Solar Panels, To Charge Our Cars (and Everything Else)," Co.Exist website (May 3, 2013): http://www.fastcoexist.com/1681413/a-road-built-out-of-solar -panels-to-charge-our-cars-and-everything-else.

10. Kaustubh Katdare, "Road That Repairs Itself—Made Possible by Self-Healing Asphalt," CrazyEngineers.com (March 15, 2013): http://www.crazyengineers.com/threads/road-that-repairs-itself -made-possible-by-self-healing-asphalt.67184/. (Note: this article includes a TedxDelft speech by creator Erik Schlagen, who demonstrates how this self-healing technology works.)

11. "Technicity—The Triumph of the Assistance Systems," *Daimler* magazine online (June 17, 2013): http://technicity.daimler.com/ en/autonomous-driving/; "Autonomous cars," Wikipedia.org: http://en.wikipedia.org/wiki/Autonomous_car.

12. Jo Ling Kent, "Driverless Van Crosses from Europe to Asia," CNN.com (October 28, 2010): http://edition.cnn.com/2010/ TECH/innovation/10/27/driverless.car/index.html?iref=allsearch; Dave Demerjian, "Look, Ma, No Hands! Automated Bus Steers Itself," Autopia on Wired.com (September 9, 2008): http:// www.wired.com/autopia/2008/09/look-ma-no-hand/.

13. See note 11 above, "Autonomous cars."

14. Susan Decker and Brian Womack, "Google Buys 1,023 IBM Patents to Bolster Defense of Android," Bloomberg.com (September 14, 2011): http://www.bloomberg.com/news/ 2011-09-14/google-purchases-1-023-patents-from-ibm-to-bolster -portfolio.html; Dylan McGrath, "Mosaid Says Google Bought Eighteen Patents for $11M," EENews.com (September 28, 2011): http://www.eetimes.com/document.asp?doc_id=1260320; Iain Thomson, "Report: Apple, Google, Microsoft Join Forces to Buy Kodak Patents," *The Register* website (December 9, 2012): http://www.theregister.co.uk/2012/12/09/ apple_google_microsoft_buy_kodak_patents/.

15. Doug Newcomb, "Google Goes to Washington to Lobby for Self-Driving Cars," Autopia on Wired.com (May 15, 2012): http://www.wired.com/autopia/2012/05/google-autonomous -washington/; see also note 11, "Autonomous cars" (in this chapter).

Here's a Google video of an autonomous car test with legally blind "driver" Steve Mahan: http://www.google.com/about/ jobs/lifeatgoogle/self-driving-car-test-steve-mahan.html (March 28, 2012). Though the test was preplanned and involved a police monitor, there was some controversy regarding its legality in the state of California. Fortunately, it all cleared in the end, and driver Steven Mahan commented that "it was some of the best driving [he'd] ever done." (Mark Hachman, "Police: Blind Driver's Trip in Google's Self-Driving Car Was Legal," *PC Magazine* website (March 29, 2012): http://www.pcmag .com/article2/0,2817, 2402380,00.asp.

16. Erico Guizzo, "How Google's Self-Driving Car Works," *IEEE Spectrum* website (October 18, 2011): http://spectrum.ieee.org/ automaton/robotics/artificial-intelligence/how-google-self-driving -car-works.

17. Peter Murray, "Better, Faster, and Cheaper—These Robots Are Invading Car Manufacturing Plants," SingularityHub.com (May 4, 2012): http://singularityhub.com/2012/05/04/better-faster-and-cheaper-these-robots-are-invading-car-manufacturing-plants/.

18. All kinds of robots are being developed and manufactured *today* by innovative companies across the globe—everything from biomedical and service robots to animal and space robots. IndustryTap.com has compiled a fascinating list of more than two hundred of these companies, including some of their robotic products and their websites. (David Russell Schilling, "Robotics Revolution in Full Swing: A Sampling of Over 200 Robotics Startups," IndustryTap.com (June 27, 2013): http://www.industrytap.com/darpa-sand-flea/3635.

19. The University of Southern California has created a virtual woman named Ellie who helps them to read the physical reactions and responses of patients—via a video feed—to create a sophisticated psychological report beyond what a human can generate. Ellie does this by asking a series of specific questions and by exhibiting well-timed, "good-listening" skills, measuring the patient's facial expressions and voice, among other key indicators. (Alix Spiegel, Your Shrink Is a Bot, How Do You Respond?" *Shots Health News* (blog), NPR.org, May 20, 2013, http://www.npr.org/blogs/health/2013/05/20/182593855/if-your-shrink-is-a-bot-how-do-you-respond.

Humanoid robots, or robotic clones, are also in the works, with surprisingly *real* results. Japanese roboticist Hiroshi Ishiguro is one who is leading the way with his Geminoid series, which includes a lifelike creation of himself: http://eandt.theiet.org/magazine/2013/09/qanda-hiroshi-ishiguro.cfm (Abi Grogan, "How Human Should Humanoid Robotics Look?" *E&T Magazine* online [September 16, 2013]).

20. Kit Eaton, "Will the Human, Non-Geminoid Henrik Scharfe Please Stand Up?" FastCompany.com (March 7, 2011): http://www.fastcompany.com/1735891/will-human-non-geminoid-henrik-scharfe-please-stand. See also note 19 above, "How Human Should Humanoid Robotics Look?"

21. Ibid.

22. Press release: "Cyclone Power Technologies Responds to Rumors About 'Flesh-Eating' Military Robot (Pompano Beach, FL: July 16, 2009): http://www.robotictechnologyinc.com/images/upload/file/Cyclone%20Power%20Press%20Release%20EATR%20Rumors%20Final%2016%20July%2009.pdf.

23. Garry Kasparov, "The Chess Master and the Computer," *The New York Review of Books* website (February 11, 2010): http://www.nybooks.com/articles/archives/2010/feb/11/the-chess-master-and-the-computer/?pagination=false.

24. Kate Torgovnick, "How Did Supercomputer Watson Beat Jeopardy Champion Ken Jennings? Experts Discuss." Technology TED Blog, TED.com, April 5, 2013, http://blog.ted.com/2013/04/05/how-did-supercomputer-watson-beat-jeopardy-champion-ken-jennings-experts-discuss/.

25. Lorenzo Franceschi-Bicchierai, "IBM's Watson Is Now a Customer Service Agent," Mashable.com (May 22, 2013): http://mashable.com/2013/05/22/ibms-watson-customer-service/; Sy Mukherjee, "Could IBM's 'Watson' Supercomputer Be the Future of US Healthcare Information Technology?" ThinkProgress.org (February 26, 2013): http://thinkprogress.org/health/2013/02/26/1637641/ibm-watson-supercomputer/.

26. Nanobots and cancer: Jesus Diaz, "This Is the Future of the Fight Against Cancer," Gizmodo.com (March 24, 2010): http://gizmodo.com/5501103/this-is-the-future-of-the-fight-against-cancer; Elizabeth Sprouse, "How Will Nanobots Help Cure Cancer?" Discovery Fit and Health website: http://health.howstuffworks.com/medicine/modern-technology/nanobots-cure-cancer.htm.

Nanobots and diabetes: Alessandra Calderin, "Nanotech Vaccine Successfully Cures Type-1 Diabetes in Mice," *Popular Science* website (April 8, 2010): http://www.popsci.com/science/article/2010-04/nanotech-vaccine-successfully-cures-type-1-diabetes-mice.

Nanobots and immortality: Andrew Goldman, "Ray Kurzweil Says We're Going to Live Forever," *New York Times* online (January 25, 2013): http://www.nytimes.com/2013/01/27/magazine/ray-kurzweil-says-were-going-to-live-forever.html?_r=0.

27. Rosa Silverman, "'Invisibility Cloak' Scientist Wins Isaac Newton Medal," *The Telegraph* website (July 1, 2013): http://www.telegraph.co.uk/science/science-news/10152577/Invisibility-cloak-scientist-wins-Isaac-Newton-Medal.html.

28. Ibid.

29. Jimmy Dunn, "Egypt: The Ancient Egyptian Heart," TourEgypt.net: http://www.touregypt.net/featurestories/heart.htm.

30. Peter B. Weber, "Neuromodulation in Neurosurgery," Sutter Health website: http://www.cpmc.org/advanced/neurosciences/bulletin/2011-1/weber.html.

INDEX

PHOTO COURTESY OF AUTHOR

When he was young, JAN PAUL SCHUTTEN didn't know what he wanted to be when he grew up: a police officer or a cowboy? Or maybe an astronaut? When he actually grew up, he knew— he wanted to be a writer, and he has been writing children's nonfiction since 2003. A native of the Netherlands, his books are popular and critically acclaimed; he has won several awards including the Gouden Griffel (Golden Stylus) for his book *Children of Amsterdam*. *Hello from 2030* is his first book to be translated into English.

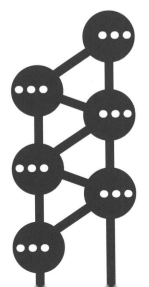